MICHAEL F. RINKER
Pioneer Pastor

Richard N. Rinker
David B. Rinker

Quill House Publishers
Minneapolis, Minnesota

Michael F. Rinker
Pioneer Pastor

by David B. Rinker & Richard N. Rinker

Copyright 2012 David B. Rinker and Richard N. Rinker. All rights reserved. No part of this publication may be reproduced, stored in a retrieval system, or transmitted in any form or by any means, electronic, mechanical, photocopying, recording, or otherwise, without prior permission of the publisher.

LCCN: 2012942354

ISBN – 10: 1-933794-53-4

ISBN – 13: 978-1-933794-53-2

Quill House Publishers, PO Box 390759, Minneapolis, MN 55439
Manufactured in the United States of America

Dedicated to the memory
of Michael and Minerva Rinker,
and the lives of those
who were touched by
their ministry

Table of Contents

INTRODUCTION
The Letter..7

CHAPTER ONE
Ancestry and Families..12

CHAPTER TWO
The Setting 18

CHAPTER THREE
The Valley and the War 28

CHAPTER FOUR
Spotsylvania Courthouse 35

CHAPTER FIVE
Post-War Changes 40

CHAPTER SIX
Decisions 46

CHAPTER SEVEN
His Faith and Religion 56

CHAPTER EIGHT
Lutherans in America 61

CHAPTER NINE
Summary of Parishes Served 68

CHAPTER TEN
Kansas, 1885-1891 76

CHAPTER ELEVEN
Eight Years–Three States, 1892-1899 87

CHAPTER TWELVE
Three States in Six Years, 1900-1905 97

CHAPTER THIRTEEN
California, 1906-1912 105

CHAPTER FOURTEEN
Final Years 1913-1930 113

CHAPTER FIFTEEN
In Retrospect 119

Acknowledgements 129

APPENDIX ONE
Bibliography 131

APPENDIX TWO
Michael F. Rinker Family Line 134

APPENDIX THREE
Rinkers in Ohio Prior to 1900 137

APPENDIX FOUR
References to Michael Rinker in Lutheran Publications 139

Index 147

INTRODUCTION

The Letter

On Tuesday morning, May 17, 1864, a regimental teamster assigned to Company K, the 12th Regiment, Virginia Cavalry, serving with the Confederate forces at Spotsylvania Courthouse, wrote home to his parents who lived at Mt. Clifton, Virginia. He was twenty-three years old. To his parents, his name was Mike, as he signed that letter. The original letter can be found in the archives of the Virginia Military Institute at Lexington, Virginia.

The battle in which his regiment was involved had begun prior to May 11 and continued until May 19. It followed hard fighting in what is now called the Wilderness Battle during the Civil War that had begun May 5 northwest of Spotsylvania Courthouse, situated midway between Richmond and Washington. Heavy losses were incurred on both sides, Union and Confederate. Michael sketched a word picture of the continuation of these battles in the letter written from his post some eleven miles southwest of Fredericksburg, Virginia. The valiant efforts of the forces he represented and the successes about which he wrote came to be overshadowed by the events that transpired at another courthouse, this one at Appomattox, less than a year later.

Tuesday May the 17th, 1864

Dear Father and Mother,

>With pleasure I write to you this morning, hoping you may get this in due time. I am well, and hope you are all well. I must ask you to excuse me for not writing sooner, indeed I am ashamed that I have not written ere this. But now I will tell you why I did not write you sooner than I did.

>We have been so busy since we came over here, that indeed this is the first chance that I have had to write. The second day after we arrived here, we commenced fighting and it is not over yet. Father, indeed for 5 days we were so busy fighting that we could hardly

get time enough to eat our meals. Today it is 14 days since we commenced fighting, and yesterday the cannon and small arms were still at work. But the fight was not real heavy all the time, the hardest fighting was on the 5, 6, & 7 and on the 9, 10 & 11 days of this month. During them six days it was awful. There was one continual roar of thunder all the time from the artillery and small arms.

For six days the Battle was kept up, all the time day and night, in the dead hour of midnight, the cannon & musketry was thundering all the time. Column after column the yankees pushed their men up to our Breastworks and our men were cutting them down as fast as flies. The dead Yankees are heaped up in piles half as high as a man, in front of our Breastworks, and all around on the Battlefield the dead yanks are lying just as thick as they can be, and none of them buried, they will all rotten on top of the ground.

Now you may know how it is down here. The line of Battle is 15 miles long, and for 4 days the Battle was kept up all along the line. The Yankees loss in killed and wounded is awful. Their loss will not fall short of fifty-five hundred in killed and wounded, and their loss in prisoners, will reach ten or twelve thousand. We have captured 12 or 15 fine pieces of artillery and 6 or 8 thousand small arms. The yanks lost in killed, 2 Major Generals and 3 or 4 Brigadier Generals, and their loss of Officers generally in killed wounded & prisoners is large. Their entire loss is very heavy, and I think it will be larger yet, before the fight is ended.

All the men say that this has been the hardest fight, since the war. It was awful for about 5 days, the cannon just kept one continual roar of thunder, day and night. I suppose you have heard, of the number of killed and wounded, of our company. You have also, no doubt heard that General J. E. B. Stuart died a few days ago from a wound received near Hanover Junction. General Longstreet was painfully wounded on the second day of Battle. But he is getting well fast.

General Lee got a dispatch yesterday afternoon from General Breckenridge stating that he had whipped and routed the yanks 2 miles above New Market and run them to Mt. Jackson where the yanks burnt a Bridge. We are all glad to hear, that the yanks have been whipped in the valley. Noah is well. We have plenty to eat. Noah give me the things that you sent to me and I am very much obliged to you for them. I will try and bring something when I get home. Tell Mother, I would like to have one pair of socks sent to me by the first one of our men that comes over. Write soon and give me all the news. I hope you will excuse me for not writing sooner, for indeed I did not have time hardly to eat my meals, we were busy all the time. I will close.

Your son, Michael F. Rinker

Our men are still in line of Battle, day & night all the time, some times they commence fighting at midnight. There is no telling how much longer the fight will last. Our men lay in our Breastworks day and night. One night last week the yanks charged our Breastworks 9 different times, and every time our men run them back, with great slaughter. If I can get time I will write to you soon or as soon as I hear from you all. I will close.

Your son, Mike

Some observations about this letter are in order. This letter from the battlefield was neat and orderly. The penmanship was good for a twenty-three year old, a farmer's boy with little formal education. This Spotsylvania letter was not written in a foxhole or trench. The writer was not huddled near the famous Bloody Angle of the engagement. The letter appears to have been written at a table. The lines are straight; the words and letters are well formed. Teamsters typically arrived and assembled around the unit headquarters. They rested and took their meals there. It is possible and, considering the letter's condition, probable that it was written while he was resting between his teamster duties. The most notable characteristic about this letter from the battlefield is its eloquence. There are spelling and grammatical errors, but the narrative flows and informs.

It was this letter written by Michael Rinker that attracted our attention and raised questions about him: Who was he? From where did he come? What became of his life? We knew some things about him because of our research into the genealogical background of the Rinker family to which Michael belonged. Additional research into his epic story, carried out over more than six and a half years, helped us learn more about him. Some gaps remain in our knowledge of his life, but we discovered many of his accomplishments. Where he lived and died are elements in his story, but we felt it more vital to answer the question, "Who was he?" As we learned more about his life, we gained awareness of the growth that took place as he matured and found purpose and a calling in life.

It is of passing interest to note that the 1850 census that included Michael's family indicated that his father, Absalom, his mother, Rachel, and all their children could read. The census ten years later in 1860, however, indicated that Absalom could read, but neither Rachel nor Hannah, a sister, had that ability. When they received his letter from Spotsylvania Courthouse, therefore, Absalom was the reader for the family, perhaps sitting around a table together.

Michael was the son of a farmer. He became a soldier, a laborer, a student, a pastor (of itself requiring the wearing of several different hats), a church-starter, a missionary, and a pioneer during his lifetime. Within his family he was a son, brother, and husband, but never a father as far as we can determine. He must have had an adventuresome spirit and a strong calling, as will be seen as his story unfolds.

Both while Michael lived in the Shenandoah Valley and while he was away in the military service for the Confederacy, history was made. In 1859, John Brown's raid at Harper's Ferry, at the northeastern end of the valley, took place. In 1861 Virginia seceded from the Union in support of the cause of the Confederacy. Two years later the nearby area of Virginia that became West Virginia was in fact removed from within the borders of Virginia and became a new state, favoring Union sympathies. Some relatives of Michael, from among the Rinkers' descendants who had come to America more than a century earlier, had property in what became West Virginia. Following the war, in 1870, Virginia was readmitted to the Union. By that time Michael had married. No trace of him and his wife, Minerva, is found anywhere in census records for that year

Michael's ancestors had prospered in this great new land to which their forebears had come. In some ways they had been unique, in others typical of the thousands who arrived on these shores, as we shall see.

As we researched Michael's life, we always hoped that more of Michael's correspondence could be found—and, indeed, more was discovered! Like the first one from the battlefield, the new acquisitions added to the portrait of Michael that was taking shape. One suspects that he wrote much more than we have been able to document. Somewhere, no doubt—in a trunk or closet, tied with a ribbon and forgotten, waiting to be found—Michael's words are there to further add to what we know about him—his hopes and dreams, his accomplishments and let-downs, his joys and his sorrows. It remains a disturbing suspicion that, when this account is published, we will encounter folks who will say, "Why didn't you ask me about this? I have some of his letters upstairs in the attic!"

Similarly, we also hoped that somewhere along the way as we searched, a picture or two could be located that would provide a glimpse of this man with whom we had developed a close—though distant in time—relationship. The first picture found, taken late in his life, is of poor quality and virtually unusable. A second picture, taken when he was seventy-one years old and living in California, raises some questions that may never be answered. Hopefully, other pictures will be found with the help of many searchers "out there" who have access to pertinent files and family records. We shall see what can be uncovered.

At the very least, hopefully, this book contributes a word picture of Michael Franklin Rinker. His character, his aspirations, his problems, his joys and sorrows, will surface as his life is outlined in these pages. Developing his life story has been a fascinating and challenging pursuit, one that has brought many uplifting moments of discovery as well as a few disappointments when gaps could not be filled. In all, Michael has seemed to come alive more and more as the discoveries have accumulated. We are grateful to the many individuals who helped make this possible.

Here, then, is his story.

CHAPTER ONE

Ancestry and Families

Michael

The surname Rinker is a centuries old German name in Europe. In this particular instance it is Swiss German, deriving from Ringger. While surnames can develop from three or four sources (occupation, appearance, father, or location), this is one of the surnames that are related to an occupation: buckle-maker in this case. The buckles in question may have been for use with harnesses for farm animals or for holding together the flexible mail segments that made up body armor.

The Ringgers who were Michael's ancestors lived in north central Switzerland, near the villages of Nuerensdorf and Bassersdorf, between Zurich and Winterthur, where the inhabitants spoke German.[1] Michael's family line has been traced back to the fourteenth century, when they lived in villages in what is now the Canton of Zurich. This is in the area separated from what is currently Germany, at the northern border of Switzerland, by the Rhine River. Uri Ringger was the earliest documented in the ancestral line; he was born about 1333.

On Sunday, May 5, 1743, five family members who were Michael's ancestors left the Parish Bassersdorf to make the arduous journey to America. The group consisted of Heinrich, age nine, and his mother, Susannah, second wife and widow of Jakob Ringger who had died in 1734 in Zurich Canton at the age of thirty-nine or forty. Also part of this group of travelers were Hans Jakob (nineteen), Caspar (sixteen), and Jakob (fourteen).[2] They were the children of Jakob Ringger and his first wife, Barbara Morff. Barbara had died in 1732 at the age of thirty-nine or forty.

The critical comments made by their pastor at St. Oswald's Chapel in the Breite community, slightly northeast of Nuerensdorf (pictured), documented in records that have survived, were anything but encouraging. Perhaps his disparaging remarks reflected the feelings of Susannah's concerned family and friends, or

12 | Michael F. Rinker: Pioneer Pastor

St. Oswald's Chapel, at Breite northeast of Neurensdorf, Switzerland. Some of Michael's ancestors worshiped here.

maybe they were primarily evidence of a narrow attitude shared by the officious clergy and church. Pastor Hans Ulrich Geszner is reported to have said:

> ... those pitiable persons who contrary to faithful warning and admonitions obstinately went away from the Parish Bassersdorf with intentions of seeking fortune in Carolina or Pennsylvania.

Zurich Canton was a Protestant stronghold. Their pastor's signature—"Pastor" rather than "Fr." (Father)—would indicate that the family was Protestant. This would mean that the family was not receiving the trip as a result of converting from Catholicism to Protestantism, as was sometimes the case, and perhaps also suggests that there was no binding indenture agreement involved, although there is some question in this regard.

The courageous spirit evidenced by Susannah and her young family, probably with little awareness of the trying hardships they were about to experience, continued to be reflected in the ventures of members of the Rinker family who came after them during the next century or more.

Accounts of similar ocean voyages described by two early records, one by Gottlieb Mittelberger in 1750 and the other by Nathaniel Ray somewhat later, combine to present a discomforting picture of what those early Rinkers endured. To begin with, there was the demanding trip down the Rhine River to the Dutch port from which their ship would embark. This trip included stops at more than twenty custom houses where passengers were required to purchase food and

Ancestry and Families | 13

necessities while they waited to be cleared at each point. When they reached the port from which their ocean-going ship would sail—either Amsterdam or Rotterdam—they were again subjected to high prices for needed goods while they waited for the trans-Atlantic journey to get underway.

Ships like the one on which they were embarking for America did not sail directly from Holland to their overseas destination; they frequently stopped at the port of Cowes, at the English Isle of Wight (near Portsmouth), to await favorable winds. It was there, too, that conversion opportunities were presented to Roman Catholics. This stopover, impatiently endured by the travelers, lasted from one to two weeks.

The discomfort of the Atlantic crossing could be made even more difficult by the presence of diseases such as typhoid fever, smallpox, scurvy, or dysentery, with all of their misery and suffering. There was little medical relief for such afflictions even if medical help had been available on board during their crossing, and that was highly unlikely. Children were especially vulnerable. It was not uncommon for families to arrive with fewer members than when they had started, bearing with them the anguish of having lost loved ones. Very close quarters, coupled with the added suffering caused by inadequate food and water, made for a miserable experience. Frightening storms and the physical discomfort of sea travel on the sailing vessels further increased the distress. Fear in the face of nature's wrath on the open ocean must have contributed immensely to the horrific unpleasantness of the experience for the travelers.

Hans Jakob Ringger, one of the Swiss travelers, was Michael's great-great-grandfather. Hans Jakob was born in Zurich Canton, Switzerland, in 1723, and died in 1797 in Shenandoah County, Virginia. At the time of his death he owned at least 981 acres of land, according to the dispensation he made of it in his will. He had arrived in the valley sometime after 1760 from Pennsylvania, because his earliest recorded land acquisition was in 1764. During his lifetime he helped a church get its start. With his wife, Anna, he raised at least three sons, and generally prospered in the midst of the valley's bounty. He and his sons grew or hunted their food, built their housing from the wood found on his land, and enabled their family to learn how to get along successfully in their new homeland. The pioneer nature of these men and women, as we shall find, continued in succeeding generations.

One hundred years later, Michael's father continued to farm in that same valley. The first census entry for his family while they were living at Mount Clifton, Virginia, is found in 1860. A decade before in 1850, however, they appear in the census located in District 58, which covers the territory around the Mount Jackson area in Shenandoah County, including Mount Clifton, located slightly west of Mount Jackson. Their neighbors were the Jewels and the Branhams. The district then, just a few years prior to the beginning of the Civil War, had a total of 12,867 white people, 271 colored people, and 911 slaves. There were 2,143 dwellings that housed 2,163 families. There were 554 farms. It was a community with common bonds, familiar patterns in their lives, and a dogged determination to build, hack, dig, and plant their way to fruitful lives with their families.

But life was not always easy. A local newspaper reports:

> We learn that, on the 3 inst. Mr. Absalom Rinker, who lived near Mt. Clifton, went out to chop fire wood, and in felling a dead pine tree, it lodged, and in his efforts to dislodge it, he was struck by a limb cutting a severe gash in the front part of his head. For several days, the wound did not seem to be fatal, but we regret to state that, on Sunday the 7th inst., he died of it.

In 1870, a year after Absalom's death, Nathaniel, his son, was located in Ashby, Virginia, with his family, according to the federal census. No record of Michael's location can be found in that year's census. Ashby is located in the general area shared by Mount Clifton, Rinkerton, Mount Jackson, and Orkney Springs, according to the atlas put together from old surveys by Lathrop and Griffing in *An Atlas of Page and Shenandoah Counties, Virginia*.

Nathaniel B. F. Rinker, older brochure of Michael

Using Lake's atlas (1885) and the 1860 federal census, locating the farm of Absalom Rinker may be possible. Although by 1885 he had died, some of the neighbors still listed on the census provide a clue as to the location. The places designated for John Eavy and Abraham Lutz on the map, and listed as near to Absalom's place on the census, suggest that they lived on the road heading slightly northeast (probably now Route 716, also known as Graveltown Road) off of the Orkney Grade (now Route 263 west out of Mount Jackson) just after passing through the village of Mount Clifton. According to the scale of the map, the distance would be about 500 rods or about one mile and a half out of the village. It would have been less than three quarters of a mile after crossing Crooked Run on that road, a creek feeding into Mill Creek between Mount Clifton and Rinkerton.

The number of Rinker households in Shenandoah County during the three decades between 1810 and 1840, just prior to Michael's birth, remained fairly constant, with only slight increases. In 1810 the Federal Census lists six; in

Ancestry and Families | 15

1820, there were seven; in 1830, eight appear; and in 1840 there were nine. The map herewith included of the area shows eight.

As already noted, Michael and Minerva do not appear in the Federal Census records for the valley in 1870. In fact, at this writing, they have not been found recorded anywhere in America. Where were they? It was a year after his father's death. His family remained pretty much intact there in the valley in 1870. Nathaniel had not yet left for Ohio.

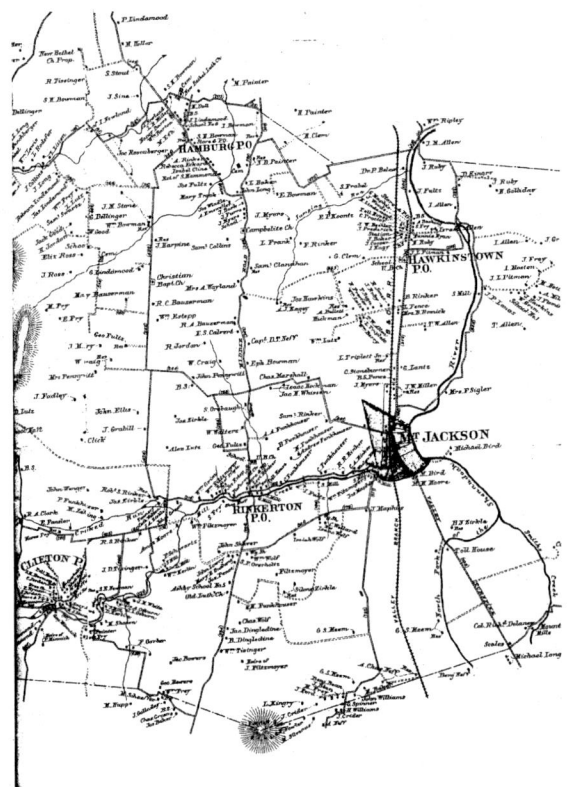

Perhaps the difficult decision to leave their homeland was encouraged by what appears to have been the loss of their father's land following his death because of significant debts. That, combined with the discouraging conditions in the valley following the destruction wrought by the war, may have motivated Nathaniel and Michael to leave for Ohio. The fact that other members of their branch of Rinkerdom had been in Ohio for twenty or thirty years may also have added to the impetus.

Minerva

Minerva Hamman was the woman who married Michael and followed him faithfully throughout his pastoral career. Alternate spellings for this surname occur: Hammond and Hammon are the most common in Shenandoah County. In the 1840 census, -an and -on appear but no -ond. In 1850, the same is true. In 1860, however, a few -an appear and many -ond. In 1870, -ond has disappeared, and both -an and -on occur, with more of -an. And by 1880, many of both -an and -on appear, with -on in the majority.

According to the census, in 1860, Minerva's home with her grandparents was only a house away from that of Michael's (living with his parents). By 1870,

Michael and Minerva had been married for about a year and a half. Michael's father and mother had both died. Minerva's father had died, but her mother, Rebecca, was living in Ashby with two of her children, Alice and Fannie, according to the census.

The Shenandoah Valley had been virtually destroyed by the Federal forces toward the end of the Civil War in an effort to cut off supplies provided to the Confederate army from that area. The promise of a better life in Ohio may have been an encouraging inducement to pull Michael and Minerva in that direction. In fact, Michael and Minerva may have been on their way to Springfield (Clark County), Ohio, when the 1870 census was taken, which is why their names do not appear in the Virginia census registry. It appears from the 1870 census that Jacob Hamman, Minerva's uncle, was living at Mad River (Clark County), Ohio. Similarly, some of Michael's relatives were in that same area and had been for a few decades—certainly an additional enticement for the young couple.

It would be difficult to exaggerate the need for the sustaining partnership that must exist between a husband and his wife when the husband is a pastor. That the pastorate took place in the rugged frontier setting commonly experienced by Michael and Minerva only increased that need. Their home was a refuge. It was a place of support where the loving presence of his helpmate provided an enduring and much-needed assurance of a calm and patient presence in his life. Together the couple grew not only in their love for one another, but also in their love for the mission to which both were called, and in their commitment to that mission with all of the sacrifices it would have required of them. If it had been otherwise, the pastor would have faltered in his efforts and their life together would have been fractured, but the home would become the calm port amid the storms of the parish. As we learn more about Michael's career, it will be seen that there were storms indeed.

Minerva died in October of 1893 at Beach City, Ohio, not long after she and her husband had left Indiana for his new charge in Ohio. Her remains were returned to Indiana for burial. Her mother, Rebecca, who had journeyed to Ohio to live with others in her family following her husband's death, died in 1898, and is buried beside Minerva at Painter Cemetery, Fall Creek Township, Henry County, Indiana. This was the area where Michael and Minerva served the Richwood (Crossroads) Church just before their move to Ohio.

Endnotes

[1] Werner Hug, *Familienchronik Ringger III* (1993).

[2] Lists of Swiss Emigrants in the Eighteenth Century to the American Colonies, 36.

CHAPTER TWO

The Setting

Geography

The Shenandoah Valley, where the twisting and turning north fork of the Shenandoah River flows northeastward toward its rendezvous with the Potomac, offers a contrast in travel styles today. If the traveler follows the multi-lane, high-speed interstate highway through the valley, the journey is fast and abounding in the sounds and habits of semis carrying their cargoes to their destinations. Travelers catch scenery on the fly, sensing that the sights may be worth stopping for a better look. But travel on the interstate isn't primarily about sightseeing; it's about expeditiously getting to wherever one is seeking to get.

In contrast, following the road that frequently parallels the interstate, Route 11—the Valley Turnpike—provides glimpses into a different kind of surroundings. Villages and towns intersect Route 11 at intervals. Collections of homes and businesses make up the pleasant communities along the way, sometimes on multi-lane highways and other times on two-lane thoroughfares. It is a route fraught with history: Battlegrounds, old buildings, repositories of stories and records focus on a common theme—the Civil War. Occasionally there is something recalling the Native Americans that once called the area home. This setting creates a natural background for thinking about previous generations of valley dwellers.

To begin to envision what life in the valley had been like, the observer must first remove modern components from the scene. Away goes the multiplicity of housing developments that can frequently be seen, developments that slice up and divide the farmland in ways the early settlers could not have imagined. Their daily lives were inextricably intertwined with the fruitful land; it provided them with food and with a livelihood once they had cleared the sections they would need to farm and live. The trees that covered the rolling hills and valleys made up their storehouse of raw materials. From them they were able to build their structures, thereby enabling them to establish their family homes, their churches, and their places of business. The rolling hills that became covered with large fields would be filled with the provender of wholesome and hearty foodstuffs. The streams of pure, cool water that flowed through it all, the animals that added their meat to the families' diets, even the sky above from which the nurturing rain came to replenish and refresh the earth and the people—all would be changed by the incursions of "progress." But when the early settlers arrived, it was a place of plenty for which they could be thankful.

The earliest European settlers did not arrive in an area bereft of people. Others had made their homes there first. There were villages and families and ways of life in the valley long before the Germans and English arrived to establish themselves. Archaeological discoveries have affirmed the continuing presence of earlier Americans. Their Great Warrior Path developed over the centuries; it later served as a basis for what is now Route 11 through the valley. The ancestors of the Native Americans in the valley had arrived from Asia over the Bering Land Bridge thousands of years before the Europeans began arriving in the valley around 1730.

In 1722 a treaty was signed between the Iroquois and the Europeans who had settled north of the valley in Pennsylvania, Maryland, and New York. Its provisions extended down into the valley. In it, the Native Americans agreed to stay west of the mountains and the Whites would remain east of the mountains. It is a fair generalization to suggest that it was not the Native Americans who first and most frequently broke the treaty. The last Native American raids on White settlements in the valley took place between 1750 and 1765. Some of Michael's ancestors may have been involved in those battles.

But the Civil War battles in the Shenandoah Valley have been well documented; these battles tend to overshadow the battles that preceded them. In 1862, General Stonewall Jackson chased the Federal troops from the valley. Again, in October of 1864, another general, Jubal Early, attacked Federal forces south of Winchester and forced them back through Middletown, routing them and driving them north. Unfortunately, while the Confederate Army regrouped and rested, a general by the name of Philip Sheridan was able to rouse his beaten troops and lead them south once again, this time to crush Early's army. The valley was never again controlled by the South during the war. The fighting seriously affected everyone whose home was located anywhere along the path of the destruction that took place.

The war brought destruction and deprivation to the lives of the valley's inhabitants. It changed lives or destroyed them. It altered what was possible for families or broke families into fragments of permanently estranged members. It caused what once may have been a thriving livelihood to become bereft of raw materials with which to work and manpower to get the work done. It created a period of shock and tragic consequences that required generations to overcome. The war was a blight more horrendous than any sickness of man, land, or beast that might smite the population of the valley. From April 1861 until April 1864 and beyond, the fortunes of the valley's people were altered in ways that could not have been imagined or expected when the war began. The family of Michael F. Rinker was in the middle of it all in that valley.

Two very different cultures found their place in the valley. One is the developed, commercialized, somewhat secularized, fragmented culture which only remembers the valley setting as it existed with increasing numbers of a non-native and non-pioneer descendant populace. The other, earlier side is the pastoral, religiously focused, supportive, family-centered and interrelated, self-sufficient culture, with its less complicated life of the last half of the eighteenth and first half of the nineteenth century. There remain some constants, however, and it is these constants that sometimes influenced Michael's life—constants not present today in the same measure, but still present none-the-less as one spends time in the valley. For example, there are still folks there who know who they are and from whom they have come. Family matters to them, and their ancestors planted the seeds from which their lives grew. Traditions still have meaning, and celebrations of those traditions can still sometimes be found.

Still today the majestic mountains remain as sentinels, as challenges, and as borders—monuments that stood firmly against too many of humankind's incursions, constant reminders of the time when those early settlers long ago dug, chopped, and dragged their existences from what nature had provided. These were the obstacles that kept outsiders from coming in without some difficulty, offering protection and security from the hustle and bustle beyond them, at least for a while.

Perhaps the most notable constant in the valley has been its impressive beauty, inspiring to those who lived within its colorful and sweeping grandeur, a source of pride and thankfulness over the generations of both later settlers and the Native Americans who settled there long before the incursions of the Europeans. Michael Rinker was born in the midst of this valley's blessings. He would later spend some of his life in areas that contrasted sharply with those early years.

Mount Jackson, Shenandoah County, Virginia, is located along the North Fork of the Shenandoah River. Mount Clifton is located west of Mount Jackson. Two roads are of importance. One, now Highway 11, originated in Native American trails running from northeast to southwest through this valley. Over these trails developed the old wagon road on which settlers traveled from Pennsylvania and Maryland, some continuing on westward to establish their homes. Later, on this wagon road, an old stage road also developed; on this same well-traveled roadbed the Valley Turnpike evolved between 1830 and 1840, later identified as Highway 11. It passes through Mount Jackson.

The second road of note was called Howard's Lick Turnpike. It headed west from Mount Jackson, through Rinkerton (yes, Rinkerton), Mount Clifton, and Orkney Springs, generally paralleling Mill Creek. A section was also known as the Orkney Grade. It became Highway 263 eventually. The distance from Mount Jackson to Mount Clifton on this roadway is about five miles. Rinkerton was the location for much of Levi Rinker's quite extensive property. He was in the same branch of the family as Henry St. John Rinker and thereby related to Michael. It was Levi's daughter, Martha Jane, who provided a detailed description of Rinkerton for Warrick Burruss, her son, who shared it with us. Just prior to the Civil War's opening forays, the village had a store with a post office, a blacksmith shop, and a shoemaker's shop. Levi's properties also included his home, his store, a grist mill, a saw mill, and a furring/carding mill between Rinkerton and Mt. Jackson. Much of this was destroyed in the burning of the valley. Michael would have been very familiar with all of these buildings and businesses.

By 1858 a different kind of road emerged. Railroad travel became possible from Mount Jackson north and east, when the Manassas Gap Railroad extended its line as far south as that town. It was the first railroad to cross the Blue Ridge Mountains. This connected the upper valley with points east as far as Alexandria and Washington, D.C. One wonders how many opportunities Michael may have had to ride this railroad.

In 1835, according to Martin's Gazette, Mount Jackson had eight family dwellings, a church, a school, a store, a tavern, a tannery, a smithy, and a bootery. Mount Clifton, down the road past Rinkerton, would have been even smaller. It had been built up largely through the efforts of the Hamman family, of whom Minerva—Michael Rinker's wife—was a descendant.

The Setting | 21

Life in the Valley

The Great Valley of Virginia is split into two valleys by the Massanutten Mountain, beginning near Harrisonburg. One segment is the Shenandoah Valley, the western most of the two, through which the North Fork of the Shenandoah River flows. The other segment is the Luray Valley, through which the South Fork of the Shenandoah River flows northeastward to its rejoining with the North Fork; together they become a tributary of the Potomac River, connecting with it just north of Bolivar, West Virginia. On the western edge of the whole valley are the Allegheny Mountains; on the eastern edge, the Blue Ridge.

The rolling meadows and bordering tree lines now seen by travelers riding along Route 263 west from Mount Jackson, past what was once the village of Rinkerton (modestly marked with a small sign), but which is now only a crossroads without the old structures, affirm the character of this next place, Mount Clifton. Named because of the cliffs that rise along Mill Creek on the village's outskirts, the structures that once lined the road have been replaced by buildings that will be replaced in the not too distant future. Some of the old houses have been moved; most have been worn down by wind and rain and snow, hot sun and the passing of time. All have lost their freshness. They contain the memories of past lives and events that changed their appearance and the lives of those who lived in them.

Where once the Hamman (with variant spellings) and Rinker families, among others, carried on their trades in structures built for business, the shadows of large, gnarled trees since grown shade the houses of those for whom Mount Clifton is now home. At the perimeters of the town and out into the surrounding countryside, a combination of old hanging-on houses and bright, recently constructed homes vie for their space and attention, the one for being so old, and the other for replacing that which was too old to retain.

In this setting, the beauty and charm of the countryside transcend the brash and the tattered. Those who really see are reminded that it was the natural setting into which pioneer settlers came to establish their legacies of hard work and simple pleasures. Using what nature had to offer them, they hacked and hewed, dug and hoed as was needed to survive. Experiencing what the valley offered them—life-sustaining springs with their promise and hope, nurturing summers with their growth, colorful autumns with their harvests, and bone-chilling around-the-hearth winters—these hardy settlers ploughed the way for those who came after them. They left their marks on the valley for future generations to ponder.

Shenandoah County, where Absalom's farm was located, had several clusters of settlements. Among them, Woodstock and Strasburg were mainly German settlements; the county was one of those with a high proportion of German families. The population increase from 1790 (10,510 people) to 1860 (13, 896), according to census figures, reflects the influx coming largely from Pennsylvania and Maryland. Reading the names of land owners in Lake's 1885 atlas of the area suggests the German background of many who had established their homes there; Funkhouser, Zehring, Zirkle, Lutz, and Dingledein are a few.

The Shenandoah County population included this large contingent of Germans, many of whose ancestors had come from Europe to escape "religious persecution, devastating wars, political oppression, and social unrest" as Wayland points out in *The German Element of the Shenandoah Valley of Virginia*.[1] As might be expected, their "religion, customs, habits, manners and language were for a long time preserved, and to this day [written in 1850] the German language is generally in use by the inhabitants," noted Kercheval in his especially helpful *A History of the Valley of Virginia*.[2]

The language of the early settlers was German because they had come from the German-speaking area of Switzerland around Zurich Canton or from an area that is now part of Germany. Michael's family probably spoke both German and English, although the census record suggests that at least one of his parents did not read or write English. This is not entirely clear. Wust, in his *Virginia Germans*, offers two viewpoints in this regard. "The [first] bilingual version [of the Heidelberg Catechism] was published in 1830 and it was used widely in the Reformed congregations."[3] And again: "In 1852, a newcomer from Germany found that the dialect [German] was still in common use among descendants of the settlers. . . . In many portions the German is yet the vernacular." Years later, as we shall see, this bilingual capability proved to be very helpful for Michael in his ministry.

Another influence on the Rinker family, particularly if Absalom's farm produced wheat, was the extension, in 1858, of the Manassas Railroad line as far south as Mount Jackson. This connected the upper valley with eastern cities and their markets. Similarly, after 1834, another tie with the "outside world" was completed just prior to Michael's birth, when the Valley Turnpike—authorized in 1834—was opened from Winchester to Staunton. It would become a key wagon and stage road.

If Absalom followed what seems to have been the most prevalent mode of farming, then wheat was a principle crop. *After the Backcountry*, by Koons and Hofstra, explains that "widespread reliance on wheat was the main cash crop in a productive mixed-crop economy." This included the need for mills so that flour could be produced and sold. "In the Great Valley of Virginia, wheat farming and the flour trade served as the main vehicles by which capitalism and its attendant values penetrated small towns and rural environs."[4] Along Mill Creek, as it ran through Rinkerton and Mount Clifton, wheat and grist mills abounded. Along with the saw mills there, industry was plentiful. Water power would have provided the energy to perform the tasks necessary to grind and saw.

Further mention should be made about Rinkerton the village, for it was there that much of the commerce took place by way of Rinker businesses. Located about a mile and a half northwest of Mt. Jackson, at the intersection of the Orkney Grade and the Middle Road, it was a place that Michael would have known well. Col. Levi Rinker, son of the Absalom Rinker who was not Michael's father, had a large house centrally located in Rinkerton. There was a Rinker's Store, owned by Levi. The Rinker flour mill along Mill Creek, five stories high, ground the corn and buckwheat raised on the surrounding farms, and necessary businesses met the needs of the farmers. Included were a blacksmith shop, saw mill, and a lumber drying kiln. The village had its own post office, and a small log schoolhouse was also nearby. Horseback and wagon rides into Rinkerton by Michael must have been commonplace.

There was, however, some diversity. Corn (the principle secondary crop), hay, small cereal grains, orchards, and timber were parts of the overall economic picture. This may have been important during the 1850s when "a glut on world wheat markets drove prices down during a period when disease and insects increasingly plagued wheat growers"[5] in the valley. It was in this setting that Michael grew up, with the joys and the hardships inherent to the economic and social culture of the time.

There was another dimension that was to impact that region and affect Michael's perspective on life in the Valley: the Civil War. Its effects cannot be overemphasized. The Great Valley of Virginia experienced the Civil War as few other areas did. Because of its key location during the War, it was perceived by the South as a lifeline and by the North as a funnel through which supplies strengthened the South's war capabilities. The one was determined to do all in its power to maintain and defend it; the other did all that was possible to eliminate it as a supplier of needed goods and as a strategic pathway to the North. Bruce Catton summed it up in *The Civil War*: "The Valley was immensely fertile, producing meat and grain that were of great importance to Lee's Army defending Richmond, and a Confederate army operating in the Valley could supply itself with food and forage from the Valley itself. ... a Federal army trying to take Richmond could never be entirely secure until the Confederates were deprived of all use of the Shenandoah Valley."[6] The valley's resources, natural and man made, were virtually destroyed as the northern troops swept through.

Prior to the actual outbreak of hostilities, the valley was neither a unanimous stronghold for slavery nor a bastion of anti-slavery attitudes. Factors that influenced the perceptions of slavery included (1) practices identifiable by national origins, (2) the nature of labor needs relating to crops and skills, and (3) religious beliefs. Michael and his family were undoubtedly affected by all three.

The census records for 1840 give clear evidence that slavery as a viable practice was maintained less in areas where a German majority existed. It was upheld in larger measure, in contrast, where English landowners were predominant. For example, in 1840 Shenandoah County (with a majority of German inhabitants) had a white population of 11,618 and a slave population of 1,033. This represents a nine percent slave component. That same year, Jefferson County (located just north of Winchester in what is now West Virginia and predominantly British) had a white population of 14,082 and 4,157 slaves. That represents twenty-nine percent. Similarly, in Clarke County (east of Frederick County, where Winchester is located) there were 6,353 white people and 3,325 slaves—fifty-two percent.

Wayland makes an observation that is worth considering at this point. The Germans, he wrote, were "taught in the habit of economy and with hands hardened to labor."[7] Their work ethic had something to do with their unwillingness to employ slaves. Perhaps in their national memory they could recall why their ancestors had left Europe: persecution and oppression. Enslaving others was not part of their makeup. The nature of what they were raising also contributed to their lack of interest in, even opposition to, slavery. In her book, The Shenandoah, Julia Davis states it quite simply: "The Germans had never considered it economical to own slaves."[8]

A major influence was their religious beliefs and the stance their churches took on slavery. Having come through Pennsylvania prior to their arrival in the valley, these families came in contact with religious groups whose position on slavery was adamant opposition: Quakers and Dunkers, Reformed and Lutheran. These traditions were upheld when they settled in the Great Valley. Unlike the Deep South, where these denominations had little presence, or even the counties nearby where German folk were not present in large numbers, the influence of the church had a telling effect when it came to the question of slavery.

This is not to suggest that there were no slaves held by any Rinker families. Absalom Rinker, not the father of Michael, in his will, for example, dated March 2, 1854, mentions a slave named Delia (*Will Book* 5, page 93). This female slave also appears as part of his household in the 1850 census records for slaves. She was fifty-four years old at that time. Absalom was a prosperous landowner in Shenandoah County. In spite of his prosperity, however, he seems to have had only this one slave. He directs his executors as follows:

I further give and bequeath to my said wife Elizabeth for and during her natural life my Negro slave Delia, two milk cows, her choice and as much of my household and kitchen furniture as she may necessarily want for house keeping. . . . If my said Negro slave Delia should survive my wife, my will is that she is not to be sold, but have the liberty of making a choice with which of my children she will prefer to live, who shall have the benefit of her services and also, support her, in case she should become unserviceable.

Notes in Passing

It should be noted here that the Rinkers associated with Michael who settled in the Shenandoah Valley were not the only Rinkers in western Virginia. At least four other groups could have been found. One was located in Loudoun County, to the east of Shenandoah County. Another was located in what is now West Virginia, in Hampshire and Hardy counties, west of the valley and not far from land owned by Casper Rinker. One evidence of connections between any of these is the fact that the Rev. Henry St. John Rinker served as a pastor at Lovettsville in Loudoun County at one point and his family lived there from 1874 until 1890, at which time he retired to the valley. Jacob Zwinglius Rinker, also originally from the valley, died there in 1916. He was a cousin of Henry St. John. A possible second connection might be suggested by land ownership held by early Shenandoah County Rinkers across what would now be the Virginia/West Virginia border. Neither of these two groups originated in Switzerland; both had ancestors who came from the area that is now Germany.

Note should also be made of two other Rinker family segments that appeared in the valley. One can be found in the family of Moses and Lydia Rinker. They lived at Stonewall (Shenandoah County) in 1870 with their five children. In 1880 and 1900 they were at Johnston. Moses was supposedly born around 1816 in Virginia, but he does not appear in earlier census records in any way associated with other Rinker families.

Another Rinker family segment passed through the valley and remained only briefly on their way west. George Rinker, probably born around 1755 in Germany, was the earliest member of this group (found to date). He had four sons and a daughter. One son, Levi, was supposedly born at Woodstock (Shenandoah County) in 1790. Other children included Elijah, Jonathan, George, and Cloah, the daughter. They were in transit, it would seem, to their next stopping place in Mason County, Kentucky. From there they moved west to Indiana and Iowa.

One of the settings, and a very special one, in which some of the earliest Rinkers prospered and had their beginnings as a family, later to spread throughout America, was the Shenandoah Valley of Virginia. To discover the early predilections of these hardy pioneers one would do well to visit the area and soak up the beauty and ruggedness of the region. At the same time, trying to imagine what was required of these folk when they arrived to establish their homes would suggest the kinds of people they must have been. It was in such a setting that Michael was nurtured.

Endnotes

[1] Wayland, *The German Element in the Shenandoah Valley*, 23.
[2] Kercheval, *A History of the Valley of Virginia*, 177.
[3] Wust, *Virginia Germans*, 143.
[4] Koons & Hofstra, *After the Backcountry . . .*, xx.
[5] Ibid., pg. xxi.
[6] Caton, *The Civil War*, 244.
[7] Wayland, *The German Element of the Shenandoah Valley of Virginia*, 187.
[8] Davis, *The Shenandoah*, 129.

CHAPTER THREE

The Valley and the War

Preparing for the War

Into the lives of those in the Shenandoah Valley came the realization that serious trouble elsewhere was threatening their way of life. Their own hard work and the sacrifices of their forebears had brought them to a point where they could begin to establish the promise of a fulfilling life. Their productiveness and the supportive community of which they were each an integral part nurtured a sense of security and accomplishment. The conditions from which their ancestors had fled slightly more than a century before seemed far behind them as they recalled their collective history. But what was ahead?

They may have been able to understand what was happening in the broad scene, though they probably had mixed feelings about what was taking place around them and why it had developed as it had. The uneasiness and the anticipation of unwanted changes that were about to be required of them must have had a disheartening effect on their ordered lives. There was little hesitation about voting when the time came to consider the Secession Ordinance that had been adopted in secret session by the Virginia Convention on April 17th: 2,513 were in favor and 5 were against it in Shenandoah County on May 23, 1861.[1]

What, then, was the response of valley men when the war came? A few, perhaps, supported the war because they wanted to continue owning slaves; their livelihood depended on having them available. Some others found the threat of the federal government's actions to deprive states of their rights more than they were willing to accept. Most in the northern valley, one would suspect, particularly those in Shenandoah County, felt their land and families threatened and were ready to defend them. McPherson, in *Battle Cry of Freedom*, cites a Confederate soldier who was captured early in the war. His Yankee captors pointed out that he was not a slaveholder, and asked why was he fighting to uphold slavery. His reply: "I'm fighting because you're down here."[2]

The coming incursion of unwanted "outsiders" brought a clear threat that was unacceptable for most in the valley. No one could have imagined the length of commitment that was to be required of them in the ensuing days, weeks, months, and years, nor could they suspect that the outcome would change their way of life for years to come. Both land workers and land owners would be affected in ways that could never have been foretold.

It is probably an accurate assumption to say that few of the valley residents, at the start of gearing up for defending their homeland, envisioned the importance that the valley would hold for the war effort that was to come. Nor could they envision the devastation that would result in their valley because of their role in the war. The supply route that developed through the valley, to provision the troops, became a lifeline, in effect. This was eventually recognized by the federal government, and they took action to neutralize this channel, as will be seen later. The war effort would demand much from the inhabitants of this fruitful land. Their sacrifices would be disproportionate because of where they were located and what they were able to provide.

A summation of the county's response to the war, in terms of manpower provided, is offered by Richard B. Kleese in his Shenandoah County in the Civil War: "Deeply partisan at the outset, Shenandoah County freely furnished her sons for the Confederate Army. Some nineteen separate commands were raised entirely within the county and over two thousand men served during the four years."[3] In what condition was the Shenandoah Valley to go to war? McPherson quotes a southern staff officer in the valley in May of 1861: ". . . the men [are] unprovided, unequipped, unsupplied with ammunition and provisions . . . the utter confusion and ignorance presiding in the councils of the authorities . . . is without parallel."[4] Those who enlisted found a lack of effective organization and a command structure that was politically appointed in most cases early on in the war. In his biography of Stonewall Jackson, Bryon Farwell paints a bleak picture of the lack of readiness: "The Virginia Militia had long been a ramshackle institution, its muster rolls a farce; men only required to drill four times a year, and often even these were neglected or turned into picnics. . . . Even at this late date none of its cavalry regiments was armed. There was even a dearth of infantry weapons and units were armed, if at all, with old muskets, bowie knives and squirrel rifles."[5] The unexpected was about to engulf them . . . and they were ill-prepared.

Among the units experiencing the lack of provisions and effective organization was the 12th Regiment of the Virginia Cavalry made up of many Shenandoah men. This regiment had come into existence when the 7th Regiment, organized in the spring of 1861, was reorganized following the death of its commander,

Turner Ashby, in June of 1862, because it had attained a nearly unprecedented size: It included 29 companies. In June of 1862 the 12th Regiment was formed with Companies A –K, which had served with the 7th previously. Three months later the 12th, along with several others, became the Laurel Brigade. More and more men were willing to invest their lives—for what they perceived early on to be a short time—in the cause that they deemed to be of vital importance for their families' futures.

Rinkers at War

The 1860 federal census provides a general idea of how many Rinkers lived in and around the Shenandoah Valley just prior to the war's onset. In Shenandoah County, for example, there were ten households listed. Just north, Frederick County had seven households listed. To the immediate east was Warren County, with four. Somewhat more to the east, and not really part of the Shenandoah Valley but closely affiliated with it, was Loudoun County, with three households. In addition, three counties in what is now West Virginia listed Rinkers: Hampshire with four, Hardy with four, and Taylor with one. These West Virginia counties were to become a separate state, but they were immediately adjacent to the valley. The total number of young male Rinkers in these counties amounted to about thirty-five (between sixteen and thirty-six years of age at the time of the census). In 1870, the census listed twenty-five Rinker men between twenty-six and forty-six years of age, the same age group that was tallied ten years earlier prior to the war's start.

Warrick Burruss recounts the involvement of one of these men: Israel Putnam Rinker (1818-1862), son of Absalom and Elizabeth (Snyder) Rinker, and Michael's uncle. He became the first commander of Company K of the 12th Regiment. During an early morning scouting foray along the Back Road, he and his detachment fell into an ambush near Zane's Furnace, southwest of Winchester. Captain Rinker was killed. He was forty-four years old and was survived by his wife, Mary Ann, and six children. Word got back to his family quickly. At New Market that afternoon, August 17, 1862, Michael and his brother, Noah, enlisted as privates in their uncle's former unit. In this same company was Jonathan Rinker, son of the Rev. Henry St. John Rinker. Nathaniel Rinker, the third son of Absalom and Rachel, served with Captain Garber's unit of the Staunton Light Artillery (Hewett). Michael had previously been a private in County F, 136th Virginia Militia; he had enlisted July 19, 1861, at Mount Jackson. On December 12, 1861, he reenlisted. The early enlistments were short-term commitments.

In the ranks of the 12th Virginia Cavalry, at least seven valley Rinkers could have been found: Erasmus F. (son of Ephraim), Fenton T. (son of Jacob

G.), Israel P. (son of Absalom), Jacob G. (son of Henry St. John), Jonathan H. (son of Henry St. John), and Noah F. (Michael's brother), as well as Michael. Several others served in other units: Benjamin F. (33rd Infantry), George (33rd Infantry), Samuel W. (10th Infantry), and Thomas J. (136th Militia). No doubt there were others as well.

The 12th Regiment, Virginia Cavalry, served in several significant actions during the war. They shared in the Maryland Campaign at Sharpsburg (Antietam). They returned to the valley with Jubal Early in 1864 following the Wilderness Campaign and participated in the Third Winchester, Fishers Hill, and Cedar Creek battles, as well as a cavalry battle at Toms Brook. Altogether this group shared in more than a hundred skirmishes and battles over the years of the conflict. Presumably Michael shared in many of them. They were at the Battle of Brandy Station on June 9, 1863, where more than 20,500 men engaged in the largest cavalry battle of the war. They captured Union railroad trains in the valley and assisted in the capture and roundup of more than 2,000 head of cattle behind enemy lines September 14, 1864, to help provide meat for the army. This action was to become known as the "Beefsteak Raid." The unit participated in the last charge at Appomattox two hours before Lee surrendered.

During his service with the 12th Regiment, Michael was assigned as a regimental teamster, beginning a few months after enlistment. This assignment was renewed in June 1863 and again in September that same year. Teamsters were responsible for the wagons as well as the mules or horses that pulled them. Their work was vital to the needs of the army. They carried supplies, did ambulance duty, and hauled prisoners. They were constantly going and coming with their loads, regardless of weather, fighting conditions, or the well-being of their drivers.

There is no reason to believe that the letter from Michael to his parents quoted earlier is the only time he wrote to them. They were undoubtedly aware of the kinds of experiences he had as he served with the 12th Regiment. Nor is it likely that the news from home to which he refers in this letter was the only time he heard from them. The fact that others from his home area were serving with him strengthens the idea that he knew what was happening back home. Indications are that a steady flow of men took place in both directions, some returning from service and others starting or resuming their service.

From the time he wrote this particular letter—May 1864—until the end of the war in less than a year—April 1865—other letters, perhaps from his sister Hannah who lived with his parents, must have brought very disturbing news as the valley was devastated and the battles slowly revealed that the Confederate Army could not match the Union Army in manpower or provisioning. Michael must have dreaded the journey back to Mount Clifton, though he was painfully concerned about what was happening to his family from day to day. What greeted him was not only the sight of such terrible destruction but also the slowly gained recognition of the list of those who had died in the fighting. In less than eight years he would leave the valley. Why he felt the need to leave is not hard to imagine. What promise was there in that familiar, but now very inhospitable, land? Eventually, with his bride, he would make the decision to leave, removing him from the place of his upbringing, good memories, and friends.

The War's Progress

Within the context of the war, Michael's letter home was sent in May 1864. In the fall of that year, September and October, the Union Army, under the leadership of General Sheridan and under the orders of General Grant, laid waste to the Shenandoah Valley. The military reasoning behind the devastation recognized the strategic importance of the valley as an attack route north and as a supplier of food for the Confederate Army's needs. As John L. Heatwole succinctly expressed it: "It was the very productivity of the valley that eventually led to its burnt landscape."[6]

From the perspective of the valley's inhabitants, the destruction of their farms —including livestock, grain storage, crops, and anything else of use that would prolong the Confederacy's ability to wage war—was unnecessarily devastating. From mid-August until nearly the middle of October in 1864, Sheridan's forces laid waste to anything that could aid support to the southern forces. Barns, mills, grain and hay were destroyed.

One man caught up in this turmoil, Levi Pitman (1807-1892) of Mt. Olive, Virginia, located between Woodstock and Winchester, was a carpenter, inventor, tinker, and clockmaker. He was also a diarist who made notes in his diary daily. He recorded those times when the war was, quite literally, in his front yard, when troops camped nearby or used the area for coming and going to wherever they were needed. It is not unreasonable to suppose that his experiences were typical of others in the valley during this trying time. Remarks made in his writing affirm that Levi was a Union sympathizer. On October 9, 1864, he describes the movements of troops near his home:

> This was truly an eventful day in Mt. Olive and our surrounding country.
>
> Early this morning scouts of rebel soldiers passed down the back road but soon returned in haste when the Yanks followed them in hot

pursuit and presently a very large force of federal soldiers appeared with heavy brass cannons, took them through our lot into I. N. Maphis's field on a high hill where they opened fire on the rebel battery which was planted on G. Coffman's hill above Tom's Brook. The Yanks soon moved the cannons high up this side of Joseph Snarr's house, soon made a charge and captured the rebel battery. The whole army soon disappeared over the hill.

The entry in his diary the day before the one quoted above offers another picture of what was happening:

> The Federal army commenced burning barns and dwelling houses early this morning. We could see dark and large volumes of smoke and still approaching nearer and nearer until they set I. N. Maphis's barn and also William Baker's and J. Rosenberger's barn on fire. They did not disturb our property.

The horrendous despoliation that took place at times seemed unwarranted, particularly when even those in sympathy with the Union suffered losses. The bitterness was reflected in the guerilla warfare by small groups of Confederate soldiers that continued during that fall after it was clear that General Early's forces, who had been trying to counter the invasion of the Union troops, had been vanquished, and that in turn led to greater efforts by the Union forces to gain control. It was six months after the destruction in the valley that Michael was discharged from service. He was released from service at Mount Jackson on April 20, 1865.

It is difficult to imagine what his reaction was when he returned to Mount Clifton. All of what he and his brothers had helped their father build was gone. With what words did his parents greet him that first meeting? With what feelings did he see what had become of his homeland? His anguish and anger can only be imagined. Friends and family members who had been fighting to defend their homes were dead. Many returned with serious injuries to a place where medical care was at a minimum or totally unavailable. Cattle and crops were destroyed; familiar buildings were demolished.

Even when the actual fighting had ceased, a Federal detachment stationed at Rude's Hill, near Mount Jackson, just a few miles down the road from where Michael's family lived, were a constant reminder of defeat, hopelessness, and emptiness in the lives of those who remained there.

Notes in Passing

A letter to Pastor Henkle at Mt. Jackson from Michael was written in late March at Brownsburg in Rockbridge County. Brownsburg is located about twenty-four miles south of Staunton which, in turn, is about ninety-five miles southwest of Winchester. Cedar Creek, where a significant battle was to be fought in October 1864 in which Michael's regiment participated, was situated about fifteen miles south of Winchester. Between the time of the earlier letter and the time of the Cedar Creek battle in mid-May, Michael's regiment was to be found at Spotsylvania Courthouse, from where Michael wrote a later letter. From Brownsburg to Spotsylvania is slightly less than one hundred miles. Therefore, Michael's regiment moved from Brownsburg, south of Staunton, to Spotsylvania, south of Fredericksburg and then back to the area just south of Winchester—all in a seven month period of time. At two of these points decisive battles were fought.

Mile after mile, through weather sometimes hot, sometimes chilling, at other times rainy, over muddied roads at times or dusty roads at other times, urging his mules forward as they pulled the laden wagon, stopping to rest infrequently as he was ordered to be where he was most needed—Michael was a team driver. He drove himself as well.

Endnotes

[1] Farwell, *Stonewall: A Biography of Gen. Thomas J. Jackson*, 13.

[2] McPherson, *Battle Cry of Freedom*, 311.

[3] Kleese, *Shenandoah County in the Civil War*, promotional material for the book

[4] McPherson, *Battle Cry of Freedom*, 321.

[5] Farwell, *Stonewall: A Biography of Gen. Thomas J. Jackson*, 149.

[6] Heatwole, *The Burning: Sheridan in the Shenandoah Valley*, 2.

CHAPTER FOUR

Spotsylvania Courthouse

While Michael was serving as a teamster with the Virginia 12th Regiment, County K, at Spotsylvania Courthouse, he wrote the letter home to his parents, Absalom and Rachel Rinker, who lived near Mount Clifton in the Shenandoah Valley. The original letter was preserved by his sister, Elnora, after their parents' deaths. Eventually it ended up with some old papers belonging to a Funkhouser family, somehow related to John Foltz, who had it in his possession at one point. It was someone with access to the Funkhouser papers who finally donated it to the archives at the Virginia Military Institute in Lexington, Virginia. That repository has graciously made its contents available.

The Battle

Michael's letter to his parents was written from a bivouac location near Spotsylvania Courthouse. The battle area where he was located is less than ten miles southwest of Fredericksburg, Virginia, and north of Richmond. The battle fought there between May 8 and May 19 was the second fought by the Army of Northern Virginia, led by Gen. R. E. Lee, against Gen. U. S. Grant as he conducted his spring offensive. It followed immediately after the Battle of the Wilderness just to the north of Spotsylvania.

The setting for the bloody battle included a trench line four miles long. At and near that line about 100,000 Union soldiers fought against about 52,000 Confederates. The former suffered about 18,000 casualties and the latter about 12,000. Lee's forces were at first successful in repelling the advances of Grant's men, but gradually Lee had to fall back and, when the battle was over, the Union forces were twelve miles closer to Richmond. In the midst of this fighting, Michael wrote home:

> For six days the Battle was kept up, all the time day and night, in the dead hour of midnight, the cannon and musketry was thundering all the time. Column after column the Yankees pushed their men up

to our breastworks and our men were cutting them down as fast as flies. The dead Yanks are heaped up in piles half as high as a man, in front of our Breastworks, and all around on the Battlefield the dead Yanks are lying as thick as they can be, and none of them buried, they will all rotten on top of the ground.

Another soldier, this one fighting with the Union Army, also wrote about the battle. His name was George N. Galloway, and he was a private in County G of the 95th Pennsylvania Volunteer Infantry. He was among those attacking the breastworks behind which Michael was shielded. Private Galloway's writings were included in Battles and Leaders of the Civil War that was published late in the nineteenth century. He wrote:

> The enemy's defenses were elaborately constructed of heavy timber, banked with earth to the height of about four feet; above this was placed what is known as a head log, raised just high enough to enable a musket to be inserted between it and the lower work. Pointed pine and pin oak formed an abatis [a barricade of cut down trees with the branches turned to face the enemy], in front of which was a deep ditch. Shelves ran along the inside edges of these works and along their flank traverses which extended to the rear; upon these shelves large quantities of "buck and ball" and "minie" cartridges were piled ready for use, and the guns of the dead and wounded were still pointing through the apertures.

Galloway (1841-1904) had been born the same year as Michael Rinker. He was decorated with the Congressional Medal of Honor for his bravery on May 8, 1864, in the same series of battles about which Michael wrote. He served from September 1861 until November 1864. His words add another dimension to the scene described by Michael:

> A momentary gleam of sunshine through the gloom of the sky seemed to add a new horror to the scene. Hundreds of Confederates, dead or dying, lay piled over one another in those pits [breastworks]. The fallen lay three or four feet deep in some places and, with but few exceptions, they were shot in and about the head.

Michael, too, remarks of the losses suffered by Lee's forces, specifically of those lost in his own company: "I suppose you have heard of the number of killed and wounded of our company." Because most of those in his company were from Shenandoah County, no doubt he lost friends in the conflict. Men continued to move back and forth between the valley and the fighting, it would seem. "Tell mother I would like to have one pair of socks sent to me by the first one of our men that comes over."

Michael, the Teamster

As a teamster, Michael probably was kept busy moving supplies as well as the wounded. When he explains the reason for his lack of communication home, he writes, "I hope you will excuse me for not writing sooner, for indeed I did not have time hardly to eat my meals, we were busy all the time." It is difficult to imagine the chaotic conditions being experienced by those on the line; the teamsters had their own problems.

Wilbur F. Hinman, in *Corporal Si Klegg and His Pard*, shares some insight into the nature of teamsters' duties: "In driving the team over the rough and isolated, poorly maintained, roads in all kinds of weather and in all kinds of desolate places, (the teamster) was constantly in danger of capture or of being picked off by bushwhackers. Since large sections of the country were woodlands, and the many valleys made fine hiding places, the hill country became the favorite haunts of roving bands of bushwhackers who were a constant threat to wagons hauling goods."[1] Hinman also describes the makeup of a mule team: "The motive power of an army wagon usually consisted of six mules. Two large animals, called the 'wheelers' one of which the charioteer (teamster) rode, were hooked to the wagon. Next were two of medium size, designated in the driver's parlance as the 'swing team.' Ahead were two small mules known as the 'leaders.' These were sometimes called 'rabbits' by reason of their diminutive size and great length of ears. The menagerie was steered by a single line, fastened to the bit of the 'nigh leader.' The driver managed the rein with one hand and his whip with the other."[2]

Teamsters typically arrived and assembled around the unit headquarters. They rested and took their meals there. It is possible and quite likely, considering the letter's condition, that it was written while he was resting between his teamster duties, duties that were some of the more dangerous during the war —bringing material and dispatches through the countryside, exposed to snipers and enemy fire while trying to control six mules and a wagon load of supplies or ammunition.

The Aftermath

Ten months after Michael had written his letter home in May of 1864, Richmond was given up to the Federal troops by the Northern Army of Virginia, and Lee led his men southwesterly to establish a new headquarters for the Confederacy. Less than a month later, the war ended with Lee's surrender to Grant.

Devastation existed throughout the areas where fighting took place, but the worst of it could be found in the southern states closest to the battles. The worst of the worst affected the Shenandoah Valley, Michael's home. The nearly total destruction of anything of use to the Confederate cause left a staggering toll on the lives of those families who dwelt in the valley. There was undoubtedly also destruction, not for military purposes, but out of the anger and the frustration of the Federal forces as the Confederate fighters refused to give in and resorted to a guerilla style of fighting to resist.

As the inevitable end of the fighting came, what must have been the feelings of those who had been fighting, whose invaded homeland awaited their return? Relief, certainly, that the war had ended. That relief, however, may have done little to ameliorate the pain of defeat and, when they finally returned home, the soul-troubling losses incurred both in property and the lives of friends and kin who would never return. Hopelessness may have been tempered by their reunions with family members, but the sacrifices made by those same family members during the latter war years especially may have added to their despair. It would be some time before reasons for hope would emerge in the valley scene.

Notes in Passing

It would be difficult to fully grasp the horror of the battlefield territory onto which Michael was called to go with his team and wagon. One account, written by a soldier who had been at the scene, is shared by John Cannan in *The Spotsylvania Campaign*:

> A legion of wounded also had to be attended to. Many of these were scarred for life by injuries from minie ball, cannon shell, or canister, wounds requiring amputation of a limb under the surgeon's saw. One Federal soldier making his way to hospitals at Fredericksburg saw many a pitiful scene as a wagon train of wounded passed him, "Many of the poor boys die in the ambulances while going over the rough corduroy roads. It was heart rending to hear their groans and cries for water without being able to help them. Those who were able to walk considered themselves lucky."[3]

Michael most likely would have shared in the transportation of the wounded.

Amid the chaos of the battlefield and the struggle to save lives by transporting the injured to the rear lines, his faith would have been tested. Two months before the battles at Spotsylvania, Michael had sought advice from Pastor Henkle about entering the ministry. We do not know the response to his inquiry. In any case, the horrors of the battlefield had the potential to cause Michael either to feel more strongly about the call to become a minister or so discourage him that he would give up his idea to serve God. That his decision eventually was to enter the ministry would seem to suggest a very strong relationship with God before he served in the war.

What we know of Michael's experiences during the war would seem to suggest that he was, indeed, a stalwart young man possessed of a singular courage. He was dependable and trustworthy in his tasks. The responsibilities he took on sometimes involved the life or death of those he sought to serve with his wagon and team. Steady nerves—imagine transporting ammunition over the rough roads—and a determination to get done what needed doing were aspects of his character. He was a steadily rugged individual.

Endnotes

[1] Hinnan, *Corporal Si Klegg and His Pard*, 97

[2] Ibid., 104

[3] Cannan, *The Spotsylvania Campaign*, 16

CHAPTER FIVE

Post-War Changes

On to Ohio

Michael was paroled from the service April 20, 1865, at Mount Jackson, not far from his home. He had traveled there following the closing hours of the fighting at Appomattox, ten to twelve miles east of Lynchburg, where Federal cavalry had surrounded the Confederate Army of Northern Virginia on April 8. If he traveled via Lexington and the Valley Road, it would have been about 150 miles.

During his years of service, Michael had become quite familiar with the devastation caused by the war. None-the-less, what he found along the way home, and what he saw when he finally reached home, must have been a shattering experience. His joy in being reunited with his family would have been tempered by the sights that greeted him: buildings no longer standing, fields despoiled, animals reduced drastically in number. Sorrow and anger, hopelessness and despair, the weary and struggling lives of those who welcomed him when he arrived back home—all compounded the brutally real facts of what the War had left those who had survived.

Not long after he got home his mother, Rachel, died, possibly some time in 1866. His father, Absalom, remarried in August 1867. Sarah J. (Sell) Rinker was his new step-mother. Less than two years after that, in March 1869, his father died as the result of injuries received in a tree-cutting accident. The incident is noted in the local newspaper as a "serious injury," so apparently he was not instantly killed. Between the time of his mother's death and his father's death, Michael married Minerva Hamman (Hammond), on March 26, 1868.

The federal census does not record Michael's location with his wife in 1870. His two brothers, Nathaniel and Noah, were listed, both of whom had also served during the war. Nathaniel lived with his wife, Victoria, and their two children, Kora and Osker, at Ashby Township, Virginia. Nathaniel and his family moved to Champaign County, Ohio, and appear in the census there in 1880. Champaign

County is adjacent to the north of Clark County, where Michael and Minerva eventually lived for several years. Noah was listed as living alone at Madison Township, Virginia, in the 1870 census. Madison was located in Shenandoah County. He married Cora E. after his first wife's death, and they remained in Shenandoah County, appearing in the 1880 census in the Ashby District.

Why was Michael not listed anywhere in 1870? The reason might have been that they were "on the road" at the time the census was taken in July 1870. Another possible reason may be the fact that the Civil War had ended just five years earlier; normal order may not yet have been restored in a way that would facilitate the gathering of census data. Census data gathering may have been hit or miss at this point. They appear on the 1880 census living in Ohio. Sometime after his father's death, they journeyed there. Michael is listed in a Springfield city directory published in 1876. So between 1869 and 1876, Michael and Minerva moved from the valley to Clark County, Ohio.

There were several other Virginia Rinkers who had moved there ahead of them. By 1830, according to the census, young Jefferson Rinker and his family had settled in Preble County, about eighty miles southwest of where other Rinkers were to follow. He was the son of George Rinker, who was the son of Hans Jakob Ringger, the immigrant. In 1827, he wed Cynthia Paddock at Preble County, Ohio. After his death, his widow and several of their children appear in the 1850 census at Brownsville, Union County, Indiana.

The 1840 federal census lists Joseph Rinker (1798-1843) living at Springfield Township, Clark County, Ohio, with his family, probably the first of the Rinkers to arrive in the area. He was the son of George, grandson of Jacob, and great-grandson of Hans Jakob Ringger, the immigrant. He married Elizabeth Frantz in Shenandoah County in 1821. In 1850 she lived in Clark County with her son, Peter, and her daughter, Elizabeth, after Joseph's death.

In 1860, Joseph's son, Peter (1824-1895), and his wife, Catharine (Weaver), along with their son, Joseph, lived at Springfield. By 1870, still in Springfield, Peter and Catharine had four children: Joseph, John, Charles, and George. In 1880, there were six: Joseph, John E., Charles W., George W., Emma E., and Harry. Both Peter and Catharine died in Clark County. Perhaps this was the family most closely tied with Michael and Minerva while they lived at Springfield.

By the 1860 census, George Rinker, son of Benjamin, grandson of Henry, great-grandson of George, and great-great-grandson of Hans Jakob Ringger the immigrant, had reached Clark County, living at Pike with his family: wife, Sarah (Branner), and children, Ann E. and John B. In the 1870 census, they do not appear in Clark County. They may be in Preble County, however, listed as

George Rungor with his wife, Sarah, and sons, Albert M. and John B. In 1880, they are again listed in Pike: with wife, Sarah, and son William B.

Benjamin Rinker (1805-1880) is in German Township (Clark County) in the 1850 census. At that time he and his wife, Susan (Zirkle), had six children: Melinda, John, George, Anna, Caroline, and Caty. In 1860, Benjamin Rinker appears in the same location living with his wife and two daughters, Annie and Catharine. In 1870, the family is still there. In 1880, Benjamin and Susanna, with one daughter, Annie, are listed there.

It is worthy of note that Rinkers from Virginia, Pennsylvania, and Maryland continued to enter Ohio following the National Road (also known as the Cumberland Road). Some of them stopped at a county along the way before moving further west to the area around Springfield—Belmont County, Licking County, and Perry County among them. One more observation seems appropriate: Immigrants named Rinker joined in the trek west. They had come from Hanover, Würtemburg, Hesse-Darmstadt, and Switzerland to build new lives for themselves and their families. Some may have been among those who helped build the new road.

Because some of the valley Rinkers had moved to Ohio prior to the war and some had been there for more than twenty years, it is conceivable that some of them had served in the Union forces. The question of whether or not they had engaged each other at some point in the conflict comes to mind.

So the valley Rinkers knew about Clark County. No doubt they also knew about the Cumberland Road (the National Highway) that ran then from Cumberland, Maryland, as far as western Ohio near Springfield. They could access it just north of the valley and follow it to Clark County, a distance of about 325 miles from Winchester to Springfield. Mule, ox, or horse-drawn wagons slowly made their way west carrying the worldly possessions of those searching for a new life in a promising territory. Michael and Minerva were among them. The National Highway went through Springfield and also through Indianapolis, where Michael would later serve churches.

What were they leaving? Of the three brothers, Noah was the one who remained in the Shenandoah Valley. Michael and Nathaniel looked elsewhere for the fulfillment of their hopes for their families. There is reason to believe—based on the numerous land sales listed for an Absalom Rinker—that the farm on which they had been raised outside of Mount Clifton had been sold in various transactions. It may well be that nothing remained for the three of them to continue farming because of the debts assigned to their father. Noah, in 1880, is listed by vocation as one who "works on farm." This may suggest it was not his farm, for others listed may use the term "farmer" when they worked their own farm. That he was working for someone else is reinforced by the census column that asks how many months of the census year he was unemployed. He responded, "One." When Michael and Nathaniel settled in Ohio, neither one took up farming. Both Nathaniel and Michael are listed as "laborers" in the 1880 census.

They were leaving an area that had been drastically devastated by the war, more so than many other places. Men who went off to fight, many of them, never returned. Civilians caught up in the battles were killed. Property was despoiled and destroyed. Funds given for bonds sponsored by the southern government were worthless. Purchases made by the Confederate government went unpaid. Hope must have been in short supply.

The Ohio Scene

This change in his location, from Mount Clifton, Virginia, to Clark County, Ohio, represented more than a mere geographical change. Their new homeland was prospering, with little, if any, of the war's ravages. He and Minerva lived in Springfield, Ohio, for at least seven years. Michael appears in the Springfield city directory first in 1876 and last in 1884. By June 1885 they were living in Kansas. Because nothing is known of their whereabouts from the time of his father's death in 1869, when it is presumed he was in the valley, it is quite possible that Michael and Minerva were in Ohio sooner than 1876. Absalom's death in Shenandoah County about a year and a half after Benjamin's birth in Ohio may have motivated Michael to leave the valley. If so, they may have moved sooner than when he first appears in Springfield, but nothing has been found in census records or any other records to support this possibility.

Clark County is located in the western quarter of Ohio, northeast of Dayton and west of Columbus. In the fifty years between 1830 and 1880 the population of the county increased more than threefold, from 13,114 to 41,948. According to population figures cited in the eleventh edition of the Encyclopedia Britannica, by 1890 the population of Springfield was 31,895, of whom seven percent were Germans, Irish, and English; about eleven percent of the people were African-Americans. Rinkers were part of that increase. What brought them there? In History of Clark County, Ohio, written in 1881, Alden P. Steele notes the following: "Taking all [the] watercourses into consideration [ed., including the Mad River and the Little Miami River with their tributaries], the county is abundantly supplied with water for agricultural and industrial purposes."[1] He goes on to say that the natural condition of the soil is conducive to wheat-raising, just as it had been in the Shenandoah Valley. Steele goes on to say that ". . . the rich bottom lands of the valleys are among the best corn lands in the country." If migrating families from the valley were looking for a good place to re-establish themselves, what better place to make a new beginning? But Michael, apparently, did not become a farmer when he got there, as some of his relatives did.

The firm of Whiteley, Fassler & Kelly is listed in the Springfield city directory as Michael's employer in 1876-1877. Michael and Minerva lived at 683 West Main Street at first, according to that city directory. In 1852, William N. Whiteley had invented a farm reaper and mower, and his company became the most important harvesting company in the world by 1887. The company eventually became part of the Champion manufacturing empire. By 1886, according to Henry Howe's Historical Collections of Ohio (Vol. I), the company was turning out a Champion mower every four minutes. At that time 2000 employees made up the firm's labor force, and the factory itself covered fifty-four acres. The firm became part of International Harvester Company in 1902, when several smaller companies merged. Michael's job description changed over the next four years, according to the directory listing. He appears as carpenter and machine hand after his initial listing with the company. Possibly these subsequent occupations continued to be with the same employer.

The remaining directory years for which records were found list Michael three more times—1881-1882 (traveling agent), 1883-1884 (no job listed), and 1884-1885 (machinist). He does not appear in the 1885-1886 directory. Their living quarters changed for each of those years, sometimes on West Mulberry Street and other times on South Mechanic Street. Michael had not chosen to return to farming. Some time later, before leaving Springfield, he made another change in what his calling would become.

Speculating on the reasons for the changes that took place for Michael and Minerva may lead to incorrect assumptions. For one thing, Michael had been a teamster in the Confederate cavalry during the war. It may have been the logical choice for him to drive a team and wagon to Ohio. Another observation: In spite of the fact that relatives in Ohio were farming, he decided at some point to work in town in an industry that served farmers. Whether or not he and Minerva went directly to Springfield and began living there or at first went where the family members had become established is unknown. Both are possible. While he was living there, he became involved in an uncharacteristic activity, as shall be seen subsequently.

Notes in Passing

The National Road, which eventually became US 40, was built a section at a time. Timothy Crumrin, in his *Road Through the Wilderness*, details the time frame within which the road was completed.[2] Begun at Cumberland in 1811, the eastern-most leg was completed to Wheeling, West Virginia (still Virginia at the time), by 1818. Once it had gone that far, renewed work did not begin again until additional funding was found, in 1825 continuing in Ohio. Four years later the project got underway in Indiana, and by the early 1830s work had gotten started in Illinois, but it got no further than Vandalia because of funding shortages and a failure to find common agreement on where it should go. It had been planned to reach the Mississippi, but it stopped short at that time.

It became, in a very profound sense, a highway of hope for those who journeyed over its wearying miles. As Michael and Minerva made their way over that highway, what thoughts must have been going through their minds as they imagined what lay before them? What were their dreams, their hopes, their fears perhaps, as the miles slowly passed? They had left good and bad memories behind. Were aspirations shared that involved Michael's commitment to a new vocation?

Endnotes

[1] Steele, *History of Clark County, Ohio*, 242

[2] Crumrin, *Road Through the Wilderness*, 115

CHAPTER SIX

Decisions

Springfield, Ohio

Michael's sojourn in Springfield seems to have been just that—a sojourn, a time between his former life in the valley and his future life which was yet to be determined. Did he expect to live in Clark County for the rest of his life? He did not become a farmer as did some of his other family members. He seemed to change occupations, possibly remaining within the same firm's employ. Did his interest in the ministry direct him to a place where a Lutheran college was located?

The experiences that had influenced him prior to his arrival in Ohio included the deaths of his parents, the loss of other family members and friends during the war, the destruction of those places dear to him, and his marriage, certainly. The conditions that prevailed and affected how life could be lived in the Shenandoah Valley must have been a determining factor. What of all that he had seen and experienced during the years of fighting during the war? Some of his words in the letter described horrific sights and sounds. Could he have not been affected by those experiences? It is interesting to note that he chose to head north when he moved—possibly because the South was in such poor shape after the war and the North was where the promise of a better life seemed to be.

Some of his family had gone to Ohio long before the beginning of the conflict that ruptured the serenity and orderly life in the valley. Their footholds—some for longer than thirty years, and the reports that they must have shared with those back home in the valley, may have influenced Michael and Minerva. His father, Absalom, along with his step-mother, Sarah, had been in Champaign County, just north of Clark County (where Michael and Minerva eventually lived) at the time of Benjamin's (Michael's half-brother) birth in December of 1867. The Rinkers there would have known of the possibilities in Clark County, not just for farming but for the industries that were beginning to develop there. It was a prosperous time, in contrast with what the valley was enduring.

Once again a journey from their historic homeland was a major decision for members of the Rinker family. The National Road ran to Vandalia, Illinois. After decades of discussion and debate within the government's leadership, construction of the road was begun by 1811. Completion to western Ohio came by the 1830s, with towns in Ohio (including Springfield) on its route. With this new avenue offering faster travel into the Northwest Territory, restless and hopeful travelers made their way over the new pathway in wagons, on horseback, and by whatever conveyance was available. To whatever degree all of these things affected his decision to leave his familiar grounds for an unfamiliar but seemingly brighter future in Clark County, Michael made the journey with Minerva, still childless, but both of them undoubtedly torn between the hope of what might be possible and the discouragement of what had been.

Nothing has been found to suggest how Michael and Minerva made the journey to Springfield. It seems reasonable to suppose they went over the new road and, because Michael had significant experience as a teamster, the use of a wagon seems a likely choice. In it they would have loaded their possessions and made their way north to connect with the National Road at Cumberland. The distance from Mt. Clifton would have amounted to around seventy-five miles using the country roads that offered an indirect route. The total distance to Springfield would have been about 360 miles. Wagons of that time could make about fifteen miles a day, depending on their load and the number of animals pulling. At that pace, the travelers would require nearly a month on the road. By the time Michael and Minerva used the road, its popularity had waned because the railroad (that had reached the Ohio River by the mid-1850s) had taken its place as the fastest way to reach into the Northwestern Territory. Some of those who shipped goods favored the railroad as their means of provisioning the large cities in the east. The supporting businesses that had thrived (inns and taverns, blacksmiths, stables, and other commercial enterprises) gradually closed down.

When Joseph Rinker reached Clark County, the frontier village that became Springfield had become a town of more than 1,000 people. Not long after the arrival of Joseph and his family, in 1839, the National Road had been completed through Springfield and that, combined with the arrival of the railroad later, enabled agriculture and industry in the area to prosper. By the onset of the Civil War, the area had become the world's leading manufacturer of farm equipment. By the time Michael and Minerva reached Springfield, the influx of migrants heading west increased the population to more than 25,000.[1]

An English Lutheran Church had been organized in 1841 and eventually located on the corner of High and Factory Streets. The church built a chapel,

Augsburg Chapel, for "missionary purposes" on West North Street in 1879, so it was present during part of Michael and Minerva's stay in Springfield. For some time previous to 1845 there was also a German Lutheran Church in town. In addition, St. John's Lutheran Church, as well as Second Lutheran Church (that later merged with others to form what is now Good Shepherd) were in Springfield. Finding out which, if any, Michael and Minerva attended has been a daunting task.

Frank D. Altman

Among all of the people and/or experiences that influenced Michael, the Rev. Dr. Frank D. Altman, a Lutheran pastor, probably was among the most influential. He was born on August 7, 1855, in Richmond, Indiana. His father was a Lutheran minister. In 1882 he was ordained as a Lutheran pastor, having completed studies at Wittenberg College in 1880 and at the related Hamma Divinity School in 1882, both at Springfield, Ohio. He wed Josephine Smith the year after he was ordained. From 1881 to 1884 he served Zion Lutheran Church in Tippecanoe City (now Tipp City), Ohio, about twenty miles west of Springfield. Records at that church do not reveal any evidence that Michael attended it at any time.

Dr. Altman taught a course in penmanship at Wittenberg while Michael was studying there. During the year in which Michael was a student at Wittenberg, the two would have come in contact, particularly in view of the fact that penmanship was one of the required courses for students pursuing the curriculum recommended for seminary preparatory students. Dr. Altman served churches at Emporia, Kansas, and Kansas City, Missouri, after leaving Ohio. He eventually went on to become the president of the Lutheran Western Theological Seminary at Atchison, Kansas. Following his seminary years, he served as pastor for St. Paul's Lutheran Church at Dixon, Illinois. Because of physical disabilities, he retired in 1919, and on October 20, 1922, he died at Lincoln, Nebraska. His obituary notice in the 1923 Illinois Synod minutes offered these observations about him:

> Dr. Altman was a bright scholar, an earnest preacher, and a faithful pastor. Bethany College, Lindsborg, Kansas, conferred the degree of Doctor of Divinity upon him in 1897. For the last seven years of his life he was completely disabled.[2]

While Michael and Minerva lived in Springfield, they met Dr. Altman, perhaps at the college, maybe at a church. In any case when Dr. Altman, who was fifteen years Michael's junior (Michael was forty-four years old at this point) accepted a call to serve a church in Emporia, Kansas, Michael, Minerva, and others from Springfield went with him. Why did Michael and Minerva move with Dr. Altman? To be part of his new parish as members? To help in the ministries offered by the church as an assistant to the pastor and as a possible beginning for further consideration of entering the ministry?

The Calling

Early in his life, Michael felt that he had been called to become a pastor. It would probably be accurate to suggest that anyone who experiences this call really has no grasp of the implications of accepting what is being offered. A cursory consideration of several of the titles applied to those who accept this invitation to serve may be helpful in understanding to what Michael was responding.

Pastor: The word means to shepherd, to nourish, to feed. Recalling the words of Jesus as they are reported in John 10: 11, those who serve as pastors are reflections of what he claimed as one of his roles among those he served. The implication seems to be that those who follow the pastor do so as sheep obediently follow their shepherd; this is seldom the case in the life of the church.

Preacher: This is probably what most people think of when they think of their spiritual leader. The preacher preaches. It is the role most commonly associated with the position. It is the title frequently used in talking about or with their leader in many places. It may also be how that person's value is rated: How well does he or she preach every Sunday, Sunday after Sunday?

Reverend: This relates to respect, being revered. The position of spiritual leader is one that is held in high regard in society, and so it probably was back in the late nineteenth and early twentieth century. This high regard did not always translate into good salaries and fine living conditions, but it did mean respect.

Minister: One who serves or assists another is one derivation. The number of different "hats" worn by the minister requires him or her to be blessed with a variety of skills, some more than others. Training helps acquire some of them; diligent development of what skills are needed is another way they are acquired: counseling, administrating, writing, speaking, communicating, conciliating, and others are required. Most ministers have both strong skills and weak skills, depending on training and interests.

Counselor: Offering counsel on a variety of subjects is one of the secondary expectations in some congregations. In others, the pastor is expected to be the "religious" expert who may or may not have guidance to offer in other fields of human endeavor. Counseling in areas like marriage or grief are generally expected.

Officiant: This is an assumed role for most pastors, but not a common title. Worship services, weddings, funerals, and other special occasions in church life require a knowledgeable leader. Sometimes the pastor serves as the presiding officer for church council or board functions. It is expected that pastors will know the proper way to carry out each function for which they officiate.

Teacher: Not every pastor takes on teaching responsibilities. One of the main differences between preaching and teaching is the role of the group being served. In the former there is usually no opportunity to respond to what is preached at the time. In effective teaching, in comparison, interaction is the rule. The one is proclamation; the other is a kind of nurturing exchange.

Father: Michael was called Father Rinker by some, at least toward the end of his life. In the Roman Catholic tradition, of course, this is common. Perhaps it was a familiar term within Lutheranism at that time as well. In any case, it suggests love and caring beyond what a religious office may require. It develops for pastors when their people come to know and love them, even as they knew they were loved. Having had no children of his own, Michael may have perceived his larger family as those with whom he served. Such an approach to ministry would be quite appropriate and one which would gain respect and devotion from those with whom he worked.

There are other titles associated with the ministry. How Michael perceived himself would be interesting to know. That he earnestly wanted to "study for a minister" as he wrote in his letter to Pastor Henkle, would suggest that he understood something of what was involved. It is conceivable that his move to Springfield, Ohio, was a deliberate choice made in order to allow him to begin his education. There is no way of knowing whether or not the choice of Springfield was influenced by the presence of the Lutheran seminary there. It seems probable.

Michael's contacts with ministers included at least two within his wider family. He knew something of what was involved in ministry. What he knew, and the calling he felt, encouraged him to become the servant he did become.

Considering the Ministry

Records at Wittenberg College indicate that Michael attended classes there during 1881 to 1882 as a member of the class taking courses in the preparatory department. The catalog for the following year lists the purposes of that Department:

The object of this Department is twofold. First, to prepare students for admittance into the Freshman class in one or the other of the regular College Courses; secondly, to provide a course of study measurably complete in itself, systematic and practical, for the benefit of those who do not intend to pursue any branches into the higher grades of the College.

It well may have been that Michael received counseling from someone at the college who explained to him the possibilities for education, both limited and expanded. Given his age, there may have been sound counsel that recommended that he not go the full route of college and seminary degrees, but that he concentrate on basic learning needs and receive a well-grounded, inclusive year of training that would equip him for his work in the field. In any case, Michael opted for the one-year preparatory course offered by the school.

The kinds of courses Michael may have taken while there include reading, spelling and analysis of words, geography, U.S. history, higher arithmetic, mental arithmetic, Latin, and penmanship (the course where Michael and F. D. Altman, who taught this course, may have made first contact). In addition, courses might have been taken in Greek and the history of England. It is highly probable that Michael did not take all of these courses during the year he attended; that he took some of them is undoubtedly true. Quite a diverse smattering of input! It seems reasonable to suppose that Michael intended to get this first educational opportunity as a basis for his later plans. Did those plans include entering the ministry of the Lutheran church?

Because of what happened subsequently, it is reasonable to assume that Michael and Minerva became associated with a church in Springfield. This was probably because their connection with a church in the valley had been a significant part of their lives. Rinkers traditionally were of the Reformed persuasion; some were Lutheran and a few were Dunkards (Church of the Brethren). Reformed and Lutheran church congregations in the valley sometimes shared the same house of worship. Michael and Minerva would probably have been familiar with both.

Two things mitigate for them becoming part of a Lutheran congregation in Springfield. The first was their relationship with the Rev. F. D. Altman, a Lutheran minister. The second was Michael's attendance, however briefly, at the Wittenberg Lutheran College and Seminary in Springfield. We do not know to which congregation in Springfield they were joined. First Lutheran Church there, after a records search, found no trace of the Rinkers.

The decision to enter the Christian ministry is not like making a decision to change jobs or find another vocation. Michael no doubt knew that a pastor was held in high esteem by most of his contemporaries. He probably also realized that he would never be wealthy or have the world's most desirable tangibles in large measure. Certainly there would be no home of their own. Customarily, pastors were provided with parsonage housing by the church being served. For churches in the process of organizing, or for those pastors serving short-term, housing would often be provided by a parishioner. The same was probably true when the supply pastor traveled a considerable distance to serve on Sunday. As he pursued his pastoral calling, moving from place to place frequently, Michael and Minerva probably did not require a large wagon to transfer their household possessions. Parsonages were usually furnished with gradually accumulating items of furniture.

He and Minerva had no children, so the pressure on their offspring was not to be a factor. Michael may not have known about the long hours, the varied skills required—especially strong and inspiring leadership, the political nature of life in the church, the expectation held by most that the pastor and his wife were exemplary models of every aspect of life. And even if he did, the call can become so strong that it wouldn't have made any difference.

Coming out of the Reformed tradition (if indeed he had), he may have found the Lutheran "style" somewhat dissimilar, but not all that much. Both Lutherans and Reformeds are confession-oriented denominations that arose out of the Reformation. Both made use of liturgical styles of worship and shared similar views of Holy Scripture, though theologically there existed some significant differences. Both came out of histories that included persecution and hardship. Both shared a Germanic heritage. Herr Pastor, for both, could be an imposing and dominant figure in the life of the church. Some of the church conflicts that later arose in some of the mid-western Lutheran churches developed because pastors were brought directly from Germany to serve in American churches, and the style of leadership provided German churches differed significantly from pastoral leadership provided by American ministers.

At what point was the decision made by Michael to move ahead in whatever ways would equip him for ministry? He attended Wittenberg College during the 1881-1882 academic year. He left Ohio with the Altmans in 1885. If he had known Pastor Altman prior to entering college, then it must have been through a church connection. Or perhaps he had gone to Springfield with the intent to begin an education at Wittenberg. Perhaps making contact with Dr. Altman was a serendipitous happening in Michael's life and with that pastor's encouragement Michael either went to college to see if it interested him or he went in preparation for entering the ministry.

He had, in fact, already made the decision to enter the ministry prior to his move to Springfield.

The letter from Michael to the Rev. Socrates Henkle, a Lutheran pastor at New Market, written March 23, 1864, asked for help in entering the ministry. This was more than a year prior to his discharge from the 12th Virginia Cavalry Brigade and the end of the war. In the letter he indicated: "This is a subject that has engaged my undivided attention for the past seven or eight years. . . . it has almost been my desire to become a minister from my boyhood."

>Brownsburg, Rockbridge County, Virginia
>March the 23rd, 1864
>Addressed to: Rev. Socrates Henkle,
>New Market, Shenandoah County, Virginia
>
>I wish to address you this morning upon a subject that has for a long time occupied my mind. And I hope most earnestly that you can and will give me some information in regard to it. I have desired very earnestly for several years to study for a minister and so far as yet have failed in it. But my hopes and desires are becoming more anxious every moment. And I do still hope that at no far distant day I may be able to realize what I have so long wished for. Several years before this unholy war commenced I applied to several ministers to aid me in my undertaking. But for some reason or other I was unable to affect much, and since I have been in the army I have not thought of mentioning it to any ministers. And so I again have thought, hoping that you will (if you can) aid me, I would like very much to commence the study at once. This is a subject that has engaged my undivided attention for the past seven or eight years it has almost been my desire to become a minister from my boyhood.
>
>I hope you will give this your special attention and tell me what you think you can do for me in connection with this matter.
>
>I will reply to your letters promptly.
>
>I hope to hear from you soon. When you write address me, 12th Va Cavalry Rossers Cavalry Brigade.
>
>Most respectfully yours
>Michael F. Rinker

Clearly his early experiences with the church back near Mt. Clifton had an effect on him. Since his mid-teen years he had given the matter his "undivided attention," as he expressed it.

One wonders why he did not approach the Rev. Henry St. John Rinker, a member of his wider family, for the assistance he was asking of the Rev. Henkle. Pastor Rinker had remained in the southern part of the Shenandoah Valley until 1874 when he accepted a call to a church at Lovettsville, Virginia, north of Leesburg. Two possible explanations seem somewhat reasonable. First, he and Minerva may have related to the Lutheran church because of her family's ongoing relationship with that denomination. It may have been his prior acquaintance with the pastor in Mt. Jackson that encouraged him to write. This would also help explain their connections in Springfield with the Lutheran school there and with Dr. Altman. Second, perhaps he did approach Henry St. John Rinker about his interest in the ministry and, though difficult to understand why, he may not have received the encouragement he sought.

The Rev. Henry St. John Rinker

While in Ohio, Michael remained employed in industry as a "traveling agent." Does that mean he was a salesman for the tractor firm? Or a mechanic troubleshooter who worked on their products after they were sold? Whatever it was, he seems to have done it while a student at Wittenberg. Perhaps he and Minerva needed that income during the year he was studying.

According to historical information provided by Wittenberg University, the original intent behind the founding of that school in 1842 was to train Lutheran pastors. He had been counseled about this decision, and it seems clear that he (and those working with him) did not deem it necessary for him to complete the full series of courses offered by the school. This kind of decision was not uncommon at that time. By the time Dr. Altman left Springfield to begin his pastorate at Emporia, Kansas, Michael and Minerva were looking ahead to taking whatever actions were necessary for him to begin a ministerial career.

Notes in Passing

It is important to note that when an individual accepts the position of pastor or minister of a local church he or she is not said to have been "hired" but rather "called." The calling comes both from the local church and from God. Throughout the Scriptures are examples of individuals who heard calls to become part of God's mission: Abraham, Amos, and Jeremiah in the Old Testament; Peter, Andrew, James, and John in the New Testament, to name a few. How and when this call is experienced varies. For Michael it finally came well along in his life, although his interest in the possibility showed up early on, probably after experiences at home, in his community and local church, in the war, and as he was in contact with mentors along the way. The measure of the call's power can be partially understood by considering the hardships both he and Minerva underwent along the way as they answered that call. They had the perseverance, strength, support, determination, and willingness to make whatever sacrifices were necessary to enable them to do their best to live faithfully in response to the call to serve. They accumulated few possessions as they traveled from one post to another. Their home was wherever the call directed them to go as local churches discovered Michael's willingness to respond and serve.

Endnotes
1 Steele, *History of Clark County, Ohio*, 414.
2 Minutes, 1923 Convention, Illinois Synod, 60.

CHAPTER SEVEN

His Faith and Religion

Early Experiences

While Michael was a child and during his youth, he was probably connected with the Reformed church or possibly the Lutheran churches that proliferated in the Shenandoah Valley. The Rev. Henry St. John Rinker (1819-1900), a prominent Reformed minister at that time, would have been well known to him. He and Michael's father, Absalom, were both fourth generation family members who descended from one of the brothers, Hans Jakob Ringger, the immigrant who had come from Switzerland in 1743. It was Henry St. John Rinker who officiated at the wedding of Michael and Minerva, probably at Grace Reformed Church in Rinkerton or possibly the Pine Church at Rinkerton, which was also the location of a Lutheran congregation.

During his thirty-plus years in the mid-section of the valley, Henry St. John Rinker served more than twelve different churches. In 1850 he was probably serving Grace Reformed Church at Rinkerton. In 1860 he was located at Hamburg. In 1870, he was back in Ashby. In 1874 he moved to Loudoun County, Virginia, to serve the Reformed church at Lovettsville until 1890, when he retired and returned to the valley, where he died in 1900. At Lovettsville community, some sixty to seventy miles northeast of the Mt. Jackson area, he would have encountered another group of Rinkers who were not related to his own family back in the valley.

During the period of Michael's early years, up to his marriage in 1868, Reformed and Lutheran churches often shared the same buildings in the valley. The Pine Church, for example, located southwest of Mt. Jackson about a mile and a half south of Rinkerton, housed both denominations until 1873. The account book for this church for the years 1840 through 1852 included the names of the Rev. Henry St. John Rinker and Israel P. Rinker; their fathers were brothers. They were related to Michael and his branch of the family by way of different sons of the immigrant, Hans Jacob Ringger.

Michael's family lived in the vicinity of Mt. Clifton, west of Rinkerton. Other Rinkers attended Reformed churches in other parts of the county. Some Rinkers were Lutheran and others Brethren. A large group of Rinkers, for example, located in what is now West Virginia just west of Winchester, were Brethren. Their ancestors had come to America from Germany rather than Switzerland. That family was not related to the Valley Rinkers, most of whom were Reformed.

Michael was familiar with the Lutherans because of their close contacts with the Reformed church in his early years in the valley. When he got to Springfield, Ohio, it may be that his contact with F. D. Altman, a Lutheran, and his brief career as a student at Wittenberg College (a Lutheran school) were preceded by Minerva's and his decision to become part of a Lutheran fellowship there. Or he had perhaps made the decision before going to Springfield, having somehow learned about the school.

When Michael began his ministry in the Lutheran church, it was after several years of contact with that denomination. While he and Minerva lived in Springfield, Ohio, they would have become familiar with a church there perhaps through the influence of neighbors, co-workers, or friends. If a Reformed church had not yet been established in the Springfield area, it would have been quite natural for Michael and Minerva to attend a Lutheran Church.

Maturing Faith

In addition to his early religious experiences and the later Springfield contacts, Michael's personal faith journey would have included some other life experiences. The war certainly would have made an impact on how he perceived himself and his relationship with God. The aftermath of the horrendous toll taken in the valley would also have affected that perception. And what of Minerva's influence? We do not have documentation of her religious affiliation, but she would have certainly been aware of Michael's interest in entering the ministry before marrying him; to become the wife of a parish pastor is not something one enters in upon without a commitment similar to that of the minister himself. It is difficult to imagine that she would not have been encouraging him.

However Michael came to the decision to commit himself to the ministry, it would have come as a result of self-examination, pondering his life's purposes, and responding to opportunities to grow in his personal relationship with God. When he was being considered for licensure and ordination, he was given the task of writing about his understanding of aspects of his faith that were pertinent to what he believed to be his calling. Would that we could read what he had written! In any case, what he wrote persuaded those who were mentoring him to accept his call to serve and eventually see to his ordination. There can be little doubt that Pastor Altman took an important role in this process.

We do, however, have something else that might be helpful in our attempt to understand what nurtured Michael's beliefs. The hymns and liturgies of the Lutheran church back then would have been expressions of beliefs with which he could identify. He did, after all, accept them as his own when he made his commitment to serve. What do they tell us as we seek some insight into his faith?

In 1880, the General Synod of the Lutheran church in the United States published a *Book of Worship with Tunes*. It was basically the preferred worship service, providing both the liturgical order along with the lyrics and tunes to accompany the liturgy. Michael would have become very familiar with this material as he led worship services.

The liturgy would have given him several things. It provided a means whereby he could bond with those he led, whether for a short term pulpit supply or a longer term interim or full pastoral service. The Lutheran tradition of theology and worship rose out of the Reformation. To be sure, it would endure further modification and refinement over the years ahead, but at heart it would enfold and value what had gone before. Although there were divisions over theological matters in the church, usually the liturgy bonded men and women in their common faith.

The liturgy also provided a statement of beliefs to which Michael could choose to adhere. Because he remained a Lutheran pastor in good standing until his death, there can be no doubt that these beliefs were indeed his beliefs. The liturgy contains the following affirmations: the Trinity, the need for repentance, the validity of prayer in its several forms, the centrality of the Holy Scriptures, holy communion, the Nicene and Apostles' Creeds, and the structure of the seasons of the year (Advent, Epiphany, Lent, Easter, Pentecost). These were the religious manifestations through which his faith was nurtured.

The liturgy pointed toward something much deeper than the printed words that were shared and repeated across the denomination. It reflected the faith relationship that Michael had with God. Experiences in his early years within his family, the horrific years of the Civil War, the deaths of his parents, the joys that came with marriage, the sorrows of the death of his life partner, and the struggles and trials as he labored to start and maintain frontier churches, Michael's faith was refined and became an integral part of his character. We cannot imagine the hardships he endured or the physical deprivations he and Minerva experienced as he struggled to share the Word of God in the primitive conditions of the Midwest and the Western frontier.

During his active ministry, Michael F. Rinker served at least twenty-four local churches or charges of more than one church in a time period of slightly more than twenty-seven years. At no point in these pastorates was he settled into one place for much more than two years. In many of them he was serving for less than one year. In those places where he was an interim or supply pastor, his time in those communities could have been anywhere from a few weeks to six months. The peripatetic nature of his ministry would have been far more demanding of him and of Minerva than a ministry served for longer periods of time at each charge.

Where did they live during these pastorates? At times he lived in the homes of parishioners, for example in Shepherdsville, Kentucky. At other times, in established churches, they may have lived in a parsonage. When he was "scouting" territories for the possible planting of a new church, he may have lived in commercial housing, for example in Glendale or Los Angeles. In any case, there had not been much time to set down roots in those communities in which he served.

It requires a high degree of commitment and a particular kind of person to continue going through life with such a transient lifestyle. It would take a person with a gift for easily getting settled in, one who could begin to make contacts without a lot of preparational time. He must have been a man to whom people responded warmly as he went about doing his pastoral work. He would have to be likeable. That was the outward person.

Minerva, of course, also had a significant role in his ministry. She created the home life to which Michael returned each day. When she was no longer with him, Michael may never have experienced the same kind of solidly grounded home life.

He must have had the mental and physical energy to continue doing daily nuts and bolts activities either when starting a new church or maintaining (at times in the midst of conflict) an established church. In addition to a wife who added her encouragement and support, Michael must have had a wellspring from which to draw, supplied by a constant faith relationship with God. It is unfortunate that we have found no writings by Michael that would help us understand something of his faith. Not every project that he took on was a success. Sometimes his situation did not achieve fruition or did not develop as he had envisaged. Not everything always went smoothly. This was a frontier pastor! Frontiers are difficult places to live under the best of circumstances.

The words that appear in his obituary from a friend probably provide the best portrait of the man:

He was a good man, keen, earnest, humble and self-sacrificing. He was clean in character, of a genial disposition, ambitious for God and the good of others. Kindness, charity and consideration for others he never lacked. He was a faithful friend, a loving, attentive pastor, and a good minister. His ideals were high, his methods thorough and painstaking. He had an unshakable and abounding faith and trust in the Holy Scriptures. With hope and joy he looked and hoped for the second coming of his blessed Lord. And in that most glorious faith he died.

Notes in Passing

The Lutheran church had clear requirements for those in the ministry. It was to these requirements Michael eventually committed himself. In its Formula for the Government and Discipline of the Evangelical Lutheran Church (revised in 1888), the following statement (Chapter I, Section 4) expresses a basic understanding of the freedom of conscience pastors would have:

> We hold that liberty of conscience and the free exercise of private judgment in matters of religion, are natural and inalienable rights of men, of which no government, civil or ecclesiastical, can deprive us.

In that same Chapter I (Section 6), the guidelines point out that those who agree on doctrine and discipline would naturally connect with each other, and they could justifiably require others wishing to connect with them to profess similar ideas about doctrine and discipline. This is clearly a common sense approach to the basis for denominationalism.

In Chapter 3, Sections 1/5, the same outline of regulatory guidelines continues, more specifically directed at the pastor and his responsibilities:

> [The pastor's] duties are principally these: to expound the Word of God, to conduct the public worship of God, to administer the sacraments, to participate in the government of the church, and to admonish men of their duties, as well as by all proper means, public and private, to edify the church of Christ.

> Pastors are amenable for their conduct to the Synod to which they belong; and that Synod is the tribunal which has the entire jurisdiction over them. . . .

> It is the sacred duty of every minister so to conduct himself that his life shall present to his congregation an example of true Christian propriety of deportment.

CHAPTER EIGHT

Lutherans in America

Developing Alignments

Lutherans in America during the nineteenth century consisted of a loosely joined or totally disassociated collection of congregations representing several different languages, traditions, and national origins, each with their concomitant qualities and differences. As the century progressed, the natural tendency of groups of people to associate with other groups of people sharing the same or similar ideas was made manifest. The result, by the end of the century, was a remarkable collection of organizations.

A comparison of the data offered by the Lutheran almanacs for 1891 and 1901 suggests the patterns and directions taken by the various groups. There were 34 synods with 1,188,376 communicant members in 1891. By 1901 there were 64 synods having 1,665,878 communicant members. During the course of his ministry, Michael came in contact with at least eight synods: East Ohio, Kansas, Wittenberg, Olive Branch, Indiana-Kentucky, Nebraska, Rocky Mountain, and California. Most of them represented geographical collections of churches.

Some synods came about as the result of language differences. Most notably, as they affected Michael, they consisted of churches wanting to retain the German language as well as others wanting to make the change to English or to retain what had already been English. This leads to an interesting question about Michael's language abilities. Was he, in fact, bilingual?

It is known that the area of Virginia where Michael spent his early years consisted mainly of families who spoke German as their primary language. The early settlers who were Michael's ancestors came from the German area of Zurich Canton in Switzerland. Others who came to the valley in the eighteenth century and shortly thereafter were from Germany. Michael, when he was corresponding to his parents in 1862, wrote in English. The 1860 federal census indicates that Absalom, his father, could read and write (presumably in English), but his mother, Rachel, and sister, Hannah, could not. Michael would have been bilingual. He could speak, and possibly write, German as well as English. Later, as he encountered churches that had a preference for German, he was able to serve them. This must have been highly desirable in some places where Lutheran churches were getting started or where they had encountered clashes in their language preferences and split.

There were other differences in preferences that affected how churches aligned. One had to do with what Phillip Schaff calls "strictness about Lutheran tradition and doctrine," as indicated in Suelflow and Nelson's *Following the Frontier: 1840-1875*.[1] Some of these early church folk were not influenced by American culture or what was happening in other denominations. They insisted on strict adherence to traditional forms and theology. These would frequently have been people who had been born in Germany and spoke the German language.[2] Others were less strict about doctrine and more accepting of other religious points of view such as the Reformed tradition, but were still interested in maintaining an emphasis, albeit less strict, on Lutheran tradition. Still others were affected by American culture, had been born in America, and tended to make use of techniques that brought into the fold some of those unchurched, i.e., revivals, and the use of English in their services.[3]

The conflicts that arose, both from religious differences and political and cultural changes, resulted in fractures within the local churches and the accompanying restructuring of church clusters with similar points of view. One synod with which Michael became engaged was the Olive Branch Synod in central and southern Indiana and northern Kentucky. C. R. Defenderfer, in his Lutheranism at the Crossroads of America, offers this: "The term 'Olive Branch' signifies a mutual concession for the sake of the mutual good held up between the two ultra parties when 'New measure' and 'Old' Lutherans were the catch phrases of controversies which threatened to rend the church."[4] That would have been written circa 1848. For Michael, this synod would have included the churches he served at Crossroads and Indianapolis, Indiana, as well as Shephardsville, Kentucky.

In 1849, the president of the Olive Branch Synod, at their Second Convention, reminded those present that "this body, as indicated by its name and motto, is based on pacific principles. Let us with equal care avoid on the one hand cold formality, and on the other hand wild enthusiasm." So records the minutes of that meeting. It must have been quite a gathering! The attitudes and predispositions represented there no doubt mirrored the feelings and dealings that transpired in some of the other synods where Lutheran churches could be found.

Language & Cultural Differences

Another such setting in which Michael was involved could have been found in the projected development of The German Evangelical Lutheran Synod of Nebraska. In 1890, a small group of members in the German Conference of the Synod of Nebraska moved to form a separate synod apart from the Nebraska Synod. They had made a request to the Nebraska Synod that had been denied because of constitutional considerations. The German Conference of that Synod had demanded "that the German Conference should have the right, on account of language difficulties, to examine candidates for the ministry, to recommend them to Synod for licensure or ordination, which act the officers of the German Conference should be permitted to perform. Further, that it should be the right of the German congregations, in matters of vacancies, difficulties, etc., to refer the same to the President of the German Conference,"[5] as it is reported in The Story of the Midwest Synod 1840-1950.

The reasons for wanting a separate identity and more control over their own German churches arose from a basic difference in the understanding of the role of the pastor and the basic non-negotiable nature of doctrine. Many of the German pastors had come to the area in response to an invitation from the German pastors seeking to strengthen their case and that of the German point of view. Non-German—and possibly some Germans who had not been born in Germany—found these pastors to be aristocratic authoritarians, impulsive, impetuous, and impatient, and with an undemanding attitude toward material support.[6]

In addition to the request/demand to be allowed to handle their own ministry needs and problems, the following were suggested as possible reasons for wanting separation: (1) American Lutheran pastors, e.g., those not born in Germany and not trained there, had a puritanical piety, i.e., non-drinkers of alcoholic beverages among other things. The Nebraska Synod, and before them the Kansas Synod, both adopted the regulation that "no Home Mission Pastor should receive any support, who drank or smoked." This, of course, included the use of wine during communion. (2) Because there was little Lutheran literature in English for pastors to read regarding theology and the church, they tended to read material from other denominations, especially Reformed. The methods and perspective of these other influences became part of the Lutheran pastors' thinking. Revivalism sometimes resulted in an emphasis that downplayed education in the church. Catechetical training was at times secondary. Union services —ecumenism in action—were also a tendency. Such practices were anathema for German pastors from Europe. (3) Open communion was sometimes adopted. This denied the need for participants to be baptized and confirmed in the Lutheran religion. German old line pastors would not accept this as valid.

(4) Lodges were becoming competitors of the church. Individuals were replacing allegiance to the church with lodge membership, sometimes because lodges made use of the Bible and religious words and phrases. The German pastors did not —could not—belong to lodges and wanted to retain the right to deny ministerial candidates standing who were lodge members. (5) There was a significant difference in attitudes toward the Confessions. The non-German pastors felt able to interpret the Augsburg Confession "as suited their particular needs at the time the interpretation was being considered. The German pastors accepted the Augsburg Confession faithfully and insisted on interpreting that confession by recognition of the whole 'Book of Concord.'"[7] There were other reasons for the conflict, including the use of the German language in the German churches supplied by German-speaking pastors who could not adequately use English. They found it difficult to participate in the life of the English language oriented Synod. Their financial situation differed from the American/English oriented churches as well, because those coming from Germany were unaccustomed to providing financial support for their churches; in Germany the state taxes provided that support. The German pastors did not encourage support.

The first German Synod meeting in Nebraska was held in September 1890 at Lanham, Nebraska. It was still not a recognized synod of the General Synod, however. At their May 1891 meeting, the General Synod laid out what the proposed new synod had to do to follow proper procedures as given in the constitution before it could be officially recognized. At a specially called session of the German Synod organizers in July of 1891, the appropriate steps were taken, and at the General Synod meeting in Canton, Ohio, in May 1893, the German Nebraska Synod delegates were seated and recognized. It was not until 1922 that the annual synodical report of this group was also printed in English.[8]

The Evangelical Lutheran Church

The Evangelical Lutheran Church in America (ELCA) came into existence in 1988. It represents the merger of three groups: The American Lutheran Church (1960-1987), the Lutheran Church in America (1962-1987), and the Association of Evangelical Lutheran Churches (1974-1987). To develop a picture of American Lutheranism during the time when Michael Rinker was serving in the Lutheran pastorate, it is helpful to note the beginnings of each of those three bodies that eventually made up the present ELCA.

The American Lutheran Church was a merger of four predecessor bodies: the American Lutheran Church (1930-1960), the Evangelical Lutheran Church (1917-1960), the Lutheran Free Church (1897-1963), and the United Evangelical Lutheran Church (1896-1960).

Similarly, the Lutheran Church in America came about with the union of four previous groups: the American (Danish) Evangelical Lutheran Church (1874-1962), the Augustana Synod in North America (1860-1962), the Finnish Evangelical Lutheran Church in America (Suomi Synod) (1890-1962), and the United Lutheran Church in America (1918-1962).

The Association of Evangelical Lutheran Churches came about when a group of churches separated themselves from the Lutheran Church–Missouri Synod in 1974. The Lutheran Church–Missouri Synod is separate from all of the above groups.

The various separations that preceded the formation of the present ELCA were based on several factors. Geography played a part, as did the national origins of those who made up the constituencies of the various groups: English (American), German, Swedish, Norwegian, Danish, and Finnish. The language differences between these several bodies were a major hurdle to unity in the early days of the Lutherans in America. And finally, there were undoubtedly theological differences among the groups. Some tended to be more conservative than others. Some were inclined toward a more open interpretation of theological and liturgical issues.

By no means are all Lutheran churches in America included in the above brief outline. Those that chose not to be included did so, again, for several reasons: national origins/language and theology, to note the most significant. Ecclesio/political considerations may also have been present in some instances, a not-uncommon factor in the relationships that develop within denominations. This might include such things as the role of the pastor as perceived by his constituency, the pastor's lifestyle, the authority of the church council (or whatever the governing body of the local church is called that includes the laity in leadership positions), the relationship between the local church and the synod or lack thereof, etc.

Within the various groups noted, the organizations that seemed to most affect the ministry of Michael Rinker are found in what became the United Lutheran Church in America (ULCA) which existed from 1918 to 1962, one of those groups that united to form the Lutheran Church in America and, later, the Evangelical Lutheran Church in America. The ULCA was formed in 1918 by a merger of three umbrella organizations under which churches and synods operated in voluntary relationships. These three predecessor cooperative bodies were the General Synod (1820-1918), the General Council (1867-1918), and the United Synod of the South (1863-1918).

It was the General Synod that seems to have included groups such as the German Nebraska Synod (when it was finally formed after the petitions made by the German Conference as noted above) and the Nebraska Synod; the Kansas Synod; the Olive Branch Synod; the California Synod; the Rocky Mountain Synod. These were not the only ones with which Michael was connected, but they represent some of the predominant ones.

Home Missions

If some of the preceding analysis gives an impression at times of disharmony, there were also times when church bodies joined together to fulfill a common purpose. One such melding of purposes is described in R. A. White's History of the Nebraska Synod: "About the year 1870 a great change took place in home mission work. Up to this time each synod had done its own work of this kind independently, and there had been no uniform plan or concerted action among the synods of the General Synod. The General Synod, in 1869, at Washington, D. C., created a Home Mission Board, to unify the home mission work, and have general oversight of it."[9] Michael would have been affected by this new board's formation.

Further reinforcement of their drive to solidify home missions as a priority at the last quarter of the nineteenth century is provided by E. Clifford Nelson in The Lutherans of North America: "During the last quarter of the nineteenth century home missions activities took priority over all other forms of church work for Lutherans in America. It was a time when enormous energies were expended in meeting and locating immigrants, in providing them with pastors, and forming them into congregations."[10]

Nelson goes on: "A man would be sent to any area where Lutherans wanted or needed a pastor. His task was to contact all Lutherans in his community and to be alert for other areas where a preaching site might be established. A small salary would be subsidized by his synod but he would be left largely on his own financially." And so, at times, it must have been for Michael.

Notes in Passing

For a significant segment of his ministry, Michael was under the auspices of the home missions boards or committees in the synods where he served. Outreach to lagging Lutherans and recruiting for new Lutherans were part of the responsibilities of missionaries in the field. The invitations involved legwork and the prospect of a new church start. The former represented an initial contact, with follow-ups as needed; the latter offered the promise of a possibility—not assured—for a new fellowship of believers including those who were contacted. Sometimes home missionaries also were used to shore up a fellowship begun by someone else and in need of reinforcement, whether the original missionary felt the need to leave or, if the charge involved more than one church, added help was required in order to effectively serve the needs of all. Michael seems to have participated in each of these kinds of situations. At times, the decision had to be made to cease trying in a given setting; the new start wasn't going to get underway for whatever reasons. This, too, was part of Michael's experience, as we shall see.

Endnotes

[1] Suelflow & Nelson, *Following the Frontier*, 134.
[2] Ibid., 211.
[3] Ibid., 21ff.
[4] Defenderfer, *Lutheranism at the Crossroads*, 47.
[5] White, *The Story of the Midwest Synod* 1840-1850, 1.
[6] Ibid., 36.
[7] Ibid., 37.
[8] Ibid., 44/69.
[9] White, *History of the Nebraska Synod*, 42.
[10] Nelson, *The Lutherans of North America*, 258.

CHAPTER NINE

A Summary of Parishes Served

Receiving a Call

When a pastor seeks a church to serve or when a church seeks a pastor, several factors are involved.

When the home missions board, for example, discovered an area not currently being served by a Lutheran church, it was customary to send out a missionary to look over the territory, perhaps do some canvassing of prospective members, and make appropriate recommendations to the board. If the interest seemed to be great enough, the board would authorize the organization of a new church start, usually with the missionary pastor getting it cranked up.

At those times when an established local church found itself without a pastor, because the former pastor had died, was resigned to accept another call, or retired, then a *supply* pastor might step in temporarily to fill in until the church could issue a call to a *full-time* pastor. If the time period was extensive intentionally, perhaps because some issues had to be worked through before a new pastor could be called, then the temporary pastor would be an *interim* pastor whose duties would extend beyond those of a supply pastor.

A *full-time* pastor might serve one church or more than one church in a charge. Charges could be two, three, or even four churches, none of which could sustain a full-time pastor on its own. Full-time pastors normally would receive a salary, a place to live, and whatever fringe benefits could be afforded by the local church(es) being served. If a local church could not fully compensate their pastor, sometimes financial aid was available from the synod in which the church was located until such time that the church could be strong enough to take over the full compensatory package.

When a local church believed it had found a person they would like to have serve as their pastor, they issued a call to that person. Ideally, the individual being considered would have had an opportunity to meet with the prospective congregation (or at least a representative group from the congregation), perhaps preach a sermon, and learn something of the needs and goals of the church. It would be of great interest to learn why Michael chose to serve the churches he did (as well as why they chose him), and whether he did not accept calls to some churches that were interested in having him serve. Unfortunately, we do not have these insights.

However, we do have a copy of the "Pastor's Call" issued by the Evangelical Lutheran Church on behalf of local churches. It can provide insight into what the "call" entails. This one appeared in the Minutes of the General Synod for their forty-second annual convention.

> **PASTOR'S CALL.**
>
> To Rev. ....
>
> Grace, Mercy and Peace from God our Father and Jesus Christ our Lord. Amen.
>
> The Evangelical Lutheran pastorate of .... being destitute of a pastor, and the stated means of Grace which God has appointed for the salvation of souls, and being satisfied of your piety, literary attainments and ministerial qualifications, the undersigned are authorized by and on behalf of the same to inform you that the said pastorate has according to the Formula of Government of the EVANGELICAL LUTHERAN CHURCH of the General Synod (Chap. 6, Sec. 5), elected you and doth through .... solemnly and in the fear of God call you to become its pastor and spiritual teacher, to teach the Word of God, administer the Sacraments, attend to the catechisation of the young, maintain Christian discipline, and perform all the other duties of the gospel ministry according to the Word of God and the rules and usages of the Evangelical Lutheran Church, your services to commence on or about 18
>
> To encourage you in the performance of the duties of the pastoral office .... authorized to promise you on behalf of the said pastorate proper attention, obedience and love in the Lord; and to free you from worldly care while you are laboring for our spiritual good, as well as to make you a suitable compensation for your ministerial services, further have authority to state that your salary shall be at the rate of .... dollars annually in .... instalments, so long as you continue its pastor, together with the free use of the parsonage.
>
> May the Lord incline you to come and labor among us in the fullness of the blessings of the gospel of peace.
>
> Given under .... hand this .... day of 18

Churches Served

It may help to note the comings and goings Michael navigated during the twenty-eight years of his ministry. When they are noted sequentially, the amount of moving he experienced becomes more impressive. In the order in which he served, therefore, these are his travels.

Michael first began serving as a *licentiate* at Trinity Lutheran Church in Greenleaf (Washington County), Kansas, on March 3, 1886. While serving there, he was ordained at the Nineteenth Annual Convention of the Kansas Synod held at Waterville, Kansas, on October 17, 1886. He remained at Greenleaf as pastor until November 6, 1887.[1] During 1887, he served as pastor for the Messiah Lutheran Church at Barnes (Washington County), Kansas, having succeeded the organizing pastor there.[2]

At the Twenty-First Annual Convention of the Kansas Synod, the organization of St. Paul's Evangelical Church at Washington (Washington County), Kansas, was reported by Pastor Rinker on March 10, 1888.[3] He resigned as pastor of that church on May 1, 1890, and became pastor at St. Paul's Lutheran Church at Minneapolis (Ottawa County), Kansas.[4] He was installed there on June 8, 1890.[5] He remained there until sometime in 1891, at which time he and his wife returned to the Shenandoah Valley of Virginia.[6] While there, he may have been associated with churches at Orkney Springs and Staunton (Shenandoah County), Virginia[7] in roles about which we have no information.

He left the valley sometime in 1892 to become pastor at Crossroads (Richwood) Lutheran Church in Delaware County, Indiana.[8] He remained there until September 16, 1893, when he accepted a call to serve the Beach City Charge at Stark County, Ohio; this charge consisted of churches at Navarre, Sherman, Cross Roads, and Beach City.[9] He remained in that area, possibly eventually serving only the Beach City church, through 1895; the 1895 Minutes of that Synod list him as supply at North Industry. He was dismissed from the Joint Synod of Ohio to go to Wittenberg Synod on January 16, 1896.[10] His wife died while they were living in Ohio, about a month after moving to Beach City. Beginning on February 1, 1896, Michael served the First English Lutheran Church at McComb (Hancock County), Ohio.[11] This charge also included the church at Malinta. He resigned from this parish January 24, 1897,[12] to serve as supply pastor for Pleasant View Lutheran Church in Indianapolis (Marion County), Indiana.[13]

At one point in its history, this church was part of the Ebenezer Charge; when he served there, it was not. He did, however, go on to serve as supply pastor beginning in October of 1897, for the Ebenezer Charge, which consisted then of two churches at Ebenezer and Decatur (Marion County), Indiana. He remained there until November 14, 1897.[14] From January 6, 1898, until July 17, 1898, Michael served the Rockport Charge in Spencer County, Indiana.[15] It consisted of three churches: Grand View, Rockport, and St. Mark's.

Michael served as supply pastor for Cedar Grove Lutheran Church at Shepherdsville (Bullitt County), Kentucky, from November of 1898 until December 31, 1900.[16] By July 2, 1901 he had moved to Saunders County, Nebraska, to serve as pastor for the Yutan Lutheran Church.[17] At the same time he also served a church at Roca, Nebraska, from which he resigned June 1, 1902.[18] He may have remained as pastor at Yutan until July 1, 1904. Although he also seems to have served sometime during 1901-1903 at Blackwell (Kay County), Oklahoma,[19] this is probably an error in reporting, as will be explained later. In September 1905 he was located in Colorado near Denver, at a place called Canon City.[20] He had been admitted to the Rocky Mountain Synod on July 5, 1904, and dismissed February 6, 1905.[21] According to the Thirty-Second Convention minutes of Nebraska, he was "engaged in mission work" while there in the Rocky Mountain Synod area.

From Colorado Michael returned to Kansas where, on February 1, 1905, he became pastor of St. Mark's Lutheran Church at Norcatur (Decatur County), Kansas.[22] He remained there until April 1, 1906.[23] During that same time, he also served St. Paul's Lutheran Church at Long Island (Phillips County), Kansas, which may have been yoked with Norcatur.[24] Sometime in 1906, Michael relocated to California, although his dismissal from the Kansas Synod did not occur until 1908.[25] During 1906 and 1907 Michael was at Stockton, California, near San FrancisCounty[26] He may also have been at Santa Clara during this time.[27] To which churches he related is unknown. By February of 1908 he was serving as supply pastor at Trinity Lutheran Church of Long Beach, in the Los Angeles area of California.[28] He remained there until April of that year. Sometime in the 1908-1910 time period he may also have served St. Mark's Lutheran Church in Los Angeles. He went on to conduct a canvass in the La Crescenta area to find out if the potential existed for a Lutheran congregation. This went on from January 16 until August 7, 1910.[29] When this did not prove fruitful, he remained in the Los Angeles area and engaged in another canvass for the Glendale section of the Los Angeles area. By September 1, 1912, the First Lutheran Church in Glendale was organized, as a result, and he served as their first pastor.[30] He resigned from that position August 31, 1913 because of health issues.[31] He remained in Los Angeles throughout his retirement.

In these nine states and seventeen counties, Michael served at least twenty-four churches, some briefly and others for as long as two years, some singly and others in multiple-church charges of two, three or four churches. Multiple churches in a charge involve even more travel than serving a single church. There may have been others about which no record is extant because of his brief supply work for them. Filling in for a week or two as needed, where invited to do so, was no doubt a familiar kind of service for him. An illness or a need to be away for a short time, for a local pastor, would require someone to step in.

About Sources

Primary sources for the information cited are of three types: The most common and most reliable, are the annual convention minutes for the various synods. These conventions were where reports were given, including the comings and goings of pastors, new church starts, the statistics for local parishes, financial data, actions of committees, and special projects. These represent the official business of the synod as reported to the synod by the various officers and committees. If these minutes have any omissions, they sometimes occur when a supply pastor serves for a short period of time.

A second kind of source for information about Michael was found in local church histories. Frequently these histories appeared in anniversary booklets. Some depended on written records kept over the years by someone in that particular church; others depended on less reliable input such as memory or notes jotted down wherever. Some presented biases, especially when the church in question had been involved in a "split" in years past. Often times pastors who served for short periods of time, i.e., supply pastors, failed to be listed. The same may have been true at times with some convention minutes as well.

A third source, and possibly the least reliable of all, can be found in the Lutheran church almanac, sometimes called the *Lutheran Almanac*. It was, at times, an authorized publication of the General Council of the Evangelical Lutheran Church in North America, and most often published in Philadelphia. In one or two instances, the data reported for Michael led to some interesting hunts; some information provided could not be validated in convention minutes.

Civil records also provide information, both the federal census and municipal directories. Neither offers a complete locating tool for Michael's movements, but they are somewhat helpful in affirming known locations at times. In a couple of census years (1870 and 1910), he cannot be found in the records anywhere.

Notes in Passing

Michael seems to have moved about often, without a very lengthy stay at a parish. For those times when he was serving as a supply or interim pastor, this is to be expected. For the other instances, it should be noted that the constitution of the Kansas Synod has this to say about moving from pastorate to pastorate in Article III, Section 6:

> Every ordained minister has the right to leave his charge and remove to another whenever he believes it is his duty to do so. . . .

The term "duty" is an intriguing one in this context. What may be implied by it? Duty to whom or what? It is important to realize what frequent comings and goings mean in terms of change and re-adaptation for a pastor. The relationship between the pastor and the parishioner is a unique one in many ways. It is a relationship that includes the high points and the low points in an individual's life experiences: birth and death, marriage and separation, as well as personal problems of many sorts, including personal faith crises. When a group of individuals come together to form a local church—a community of faith—it is not always enough to know that God loves them. There will be differences and disagreements, religious/political preferences, and opinions about what should be happening, who has a position of power, and who will fill which important roles in the life of that church. The old-timers and the new-comers sometimes fail to see eye to eye on some matters. The pastor must minister to both. The need for retaining "the way it's always been" and being able to adapt with changes to meet new challenges and opportunities can be a source of divisive conflicts. Reconciliation and counseling are aspects of the pastor's vocation that demand much of the pastor's personal strength and faith. It would seem that Michael rarely had time in any given setting to enjoy the fruits of his labor. That he was effective in what he did cannot be doubted; he continued to be assigned or called.

The travel component should also be considered, with no superhighways over which to speed to the next assignment by auto. There may have been train service available or in some cases riverboat service. That there were horse or mule drawn wagons, and horseback riding, is certain. In rural settings, distances between parishioners' homes could be considerable. Sickness and family problems requiring visits by the pastor meant travel time in the saddle. There were few hospitals centrally located on the frontier; health care was usually in the homes. Meals were taken as they were made available. At one point in his ministry, Michael submitted his resignation as pastor because he could no longer endure the horseback travel that he had been required to do in order to serve his parishioners.

As one examines the list of parishes served by Michael Rinker, the question arises: Why did Michael not remain for longer periods of time at the churches he served? Remarks reporting his service such as "Rev. Rinker served the congregation (McComb, Ohio) but a year and then resigned," may suggest surprise or disappointment that he left so soon. Does the fact of his short stays reflect his lack of preparation? The nature of the situations into which he moved? The specific need being felt by a church to which he had been called to minister and his subsequent accomplishment of that task? His personal wander lust? Something about his character that made it difficult for him to remain? Dissatisfaction felt by those with whom he ministered? His own financial needs that weren't being met? Or a specific kind of ministry that brought him in contact with churches for intentionally short periods of time, churches with specific problems or needs to which he could address himself and respond to over a relatively short period of time?

Statistical tables reported by synods in which Michael served show that Michael served churches ranging in membership size from sixteen to sixty-six. He served five churches with memberships between sixteen and twenty; eleven churches between twenty-one and forty; nine churches exceeding forty members.

Michael lived to be nearly ninety years old! Quite a feat in those times and in light of the nature of his lifestyle while ministering to his congregations.

Endnotes

[1] Minutes, Nineteenth Annual Convention, Kansas Synod, 8.

[2] Ibid, 31.

[3] Minutes, Twenty-first Annual Convention, Kansas Synod, 8.

[4] *A History of the Evangelical Synod of Kansas*, 189.

[5] Minutes, Twenty-first Annual Convention, Kansas Synod, 9.

[6] *A History of the Evangelical Lutheran Synod of Kansas*, 124.

[7] Minutes, Twenty-third Annual Convention, Kansas Synod, 124.

[8] Minutes, Twenty-fourth Annual Convention, Kansas Synod, 7.

[9] 1892 *Lutheran Almanac*, 47.

[10] 150th anniversary booklet, First Lutheran Church of Cross Roads.

[11] Minutes, 1894 East Ohio Synod, 32.

[12] Minutes, 1896 East Ohio Synod, 42.

[13] Minutes, Fiftieth Annual Convention, Wittenberg Synod, 10.

[14] Minutes, 1897 Annual Convention, Wittenberg Synod, 11.

[15] 100th anniversary booklet, Pleasant View English Lutheran Church.

[16] Minutes, 1898 Annual Convention, Olive Branch Synod, 6.

[17] Centennial anniversary booklet, St. Mark's Lutheran Church.

[18] Minutes, 1899 Olive Branch Synod, 9.

[19] Minutes, Fifty-fourth Annual Convention, Olive Branch Synod, 7.

[20] Minutes, Thirtieth Annual Convention, Nebraska Synod, 5.

[21] *Lutheran Almanac* (1902), 48.

[22] Minutes, Thirty-eighth Annual Convention, Kansas Synod, 8.

[23] Minutes, Thirty-ninth Annual Convention, Kansas Synod, 7.

[24] *History of St. Paul's Lutheran Church*.

[25] Minutes, Forty-first Annual Convention, Kansas Synod, 9.
[26] *Lutheran Almanac* (1907), 82.
[27] *Lutheran Almanac* (1908), 84.
[28] Minutes, Eighteenth Annual Convention, California Synod, 14.
[29] Minutes, Twenty-first Annual Convention, California Synod, 22.
[30] Minutes, Twenty-second Annual Convention, California Synod, 10.
[31] Minutes, Twenty-third Annual Convention, California Synod, 8.

CHAPTER TEN

Kansas
1885-1891

Emporia

It seems certain that Michael had continued thinking about entering the ministry while still in Springfield, Ohio. It also is conceivable that Pastor Altman was able to put him to work in some capacity at St. Mark's Lutheran Church at Emporia. It is known, from a newspaper article in the summer of 1885, that he was named to be one of the church's first deacons as soon as St. Mark's was organized.

> Sunday the St. Mark's Lutheran Church of Emporia was organized by Rev. F. D. Altman at the Reformed Church building, on the corner of Ninth and Constitution Streets. The elders chosen are W. W. Kremer and J. Fulmer. The deacons are Alfred Nicholas, George Balner, M. F. Rinker, Lawrence Boorey. It is the object of the congregation to keep an outlook for suitable lots, and build a church edifice as soon as convenient" (*Emporia Weekly News*, June 25, 1885).

The 1890 edition of Formula for the Government and Discipline of the Evangelical Lutheran Church of the General Synod in the United States offers this for deacons' responsibilities:

> to lead an exemplary life . . . to minister unto the poor, extending to their wants and distributing faithfully amongst them the collections which may be made for their use . . . to assist the pastor in the administration of the Eucharist . . . to attend and render all necessary service at stated worship . . . to see that their minister receives a just and adequate support . . . to administer the temporal concerns of the church.[1]

Certainly, good practice for the ministry!

He may have shared in Sunday school responsibilities. Dr. Altman wasted no time in organizing for the church's educational needs, organizing the Sunday school by June 14, 1885, two weeks after beginning his work there, according to Ott's *History of the Kansas Synod*. On two occasions his name was mentioned in the local Emporia newspapers in connection with attendance at Sunday school conventions (May 1886 and February 1890). Perhaps Michael was encouraged to try his hand at preaching. It somehow seems unreasonable to suppose that he did nothing along this line if his intent was to become a pastor.

Kansas, where Michael began his ministry and to which he returned later, was in a prime location, geographically and historically, for turmoil and turbulence just before the Civil War. Its motto, *Ad Astra per Aspera* (to the stars through difficulties) about sums up its journey to statehood in January 1861. Adolph Roenigh, in his *Pioneer History of Kansas*, elaborates:

> As though the manifold dangers of Indians, desperadoes, and freebooters (plunderers) were not enough to embarrass the settlement of a new land, the sable cloud of slavery must push its dark shadow over the sunny plains of Kansas. Some of the noblest, and certainly many of the most evil qualities of men, were brought out in the contest for freedom or liberty for the black, which be said to have begun with the agitation resulting in the Missouri Compromise and ending only with the last shot of the Civil War.[2]

Kansas was torn apart in the struggle that resulted in that territory when pro- and anti-slavery forces struggled bloodily to win their cause.

Twenty years after the end of the war, the Rev. F. D. Altman and those who accompanied him from Springfield, Ohio, came to Emporia, Kansas, located midway between Topeka and Wichita in the eastern part of the state in Lyon County. How he came to be there is related in the book by the Rev. H. A. Ott, *A History of the Evangelical Lutheran Synod of Kansas*, published in 1907. The initial effort to organize a church in Emporia was unsuccessful because "the Missionary Board could neither furnish aid nor a minister to take care of the field," quoting from a report made by the synod president. Ott goes on: "However in 1883-84 the Synodical pressure on the Mission Board to send a man into this city became so imperious that the Board acted. . . ." and a man was called to serve. After five months, however, "not liking the West," he resigned.[3]

"In April the following year a call was extended to Rev. F. D. Altman, of Tippecanoe City, Ohio, as missionary, who began operations June 13." He soon reorganized the congregation; Mr. and Mrs. M. F. Rinker were among the members. The use of the facilities of the Reformed Church were shared with the fledging group and they held services twice every Sunday, as well as a Sunday school that was soon organized. That was the beginning of what would become St. Mark's Lutheran Church.

Pastor Altman was commended for his efforts. He had taken on the assignment for the board for home missions on May 26. In the minutes of their Eighteenth Annual Convention, the report on new church starts included: "Rev. F. D. Altman organized the Emporia mission in June last with twenty-two members. The work is growing and commendable steps have been taken to secure their own house of worship."[4]

What was Emporia like in 1885? By 1880 it had a population of 7,100 in the city and surrounding township, after small beginnings in February 1857 when a few men began leading the development of the area. One of the principal founders was from Ohio. Settlers began arriving soon after, and by 1865 it became recognized as a village. By 1870 it was incorporated as a second class city. The railroad arrived at the end of 1860 (the M. K. & T.) and expanded by mid-1870 (the A.T. & S. F.). These bits and pieces of data are from William G. Cutler's *A History of the State of Kansas*. In describing the county in which Emporia is located, the author reports fifteen percent bottomland, eighty-five percent forest, and eight percent prairie. The book was written in 1883 and, as would be expected, Cutler's list of churches did not include a Lutheran church among the several listed.

Entering the Ministry

The first step in becoming officially recognized as a pastor in this Lutheran denomination was called licensure. The constitution of the Kansas Synod briefly describes the process involved in Article IX[5]:

> Sec. 4. A Committee of three shall be annually appointed on Beneficiary Education, who shall receive applications for aid, examine the applicants, recommend the amount of aid to be given to each, and render an annual report to Synod of all their action in the matters pertaining to Beneficiary Education.

> Sec. 5. There shall be an Examining Committee of five ordained ministers appointed annually, whose duty it shall be to examine candidates for licensure and ordination. As these examinations may be highly interesting and useful to the whole Ministerium, and will be more faithfully performed if public, it is earnestly recommended that they be performed before the whole body.

> Sec. 6. After the examination by the Committee is ended, every member of the Ministerium has the right to ask the applicant any additional questions.

Sec. 7. The examination shall embrace at least the following subjects: personal Piety and of the motives of the applicant for seeking the holy office, the Greek and Hebrew Scriptures, the Evidences of Christianity, Natural and Revealed Theology, Church History, Pastoral Theology, the rules of Sermonizing and Church government.

Sec. 8. No Ministerium shall, in any case whatever, license an individual whom they do not believe to be hopefully pious. Nor shall any applicant, extraordinary cases excepted, be licensed, whom the Ministerium do not find possessed of a competent acquaintance with the subjects named in Section 7, the Hebrew language alone excepted.

Sec. 9. The Ceremony of Licensure shall be performed according to the Liturgy of the Church.

Article III, Section 10, also states this about the licentiate:

Every licentiate must keep a journal of his ministerial acts, which with a few sermons of his own composition, he must deliver, or send annually for the inspection of the Ministerium.

If a candidate who has been licensed for an appropriate period of time (Licensure is ordinarily renewed annually), and if he has been found to be a qualified candidate then the next step would be full ordination. The constitution goes on to say:

Sec. 11. If a licentiate, after some time of probation, does, in the judgment of the Ministerium, prove himself unqualified for the duties of the ministry, his license shall be withdrawn.

Sec. 12. Whenever the Ministerium has decided that an individual shall be ordained, the ceremony may be performed, either at the time, by the assembled Ministerium, or, if preferred, in the church by which he has been called, by the Special Conference, or by a committee appointed for the purpose by the (Synod) President. The ceremony of Ordination, wherever performed, shall be according to the Liturgy of the Church.[5]

It was not long after arriving at Emporia that Michael began taking the steps necessary to become a Lutheran minister. This would seem to suggest that he had been contemplating this decision prior to his arrival in Kansas. In mid-September 1885 he wrote to the synod requesting consideration for licensure.

After applying for licensure, Michael met with those responsible for granting entry into the process and was required to submit some evidences of his abilities and commitment. The minutes of the Eighteenth Annual Convention of the Kansas Evangelical Lutheran Synod held at Peabody, Kansas, reported two items relating to him. The first:

> There have been placed in our (Executive Committee of the Ministerium) hands two manuscripts by Mr. M. F. Rinker, of Emporia, Kansas, which are designed to illustrate his method of handling the Word of God for the edification of souls. We have also had a colloquium with Bro. Rinker, with a view to his licensure. We recommend that he be licensed for one year, believing that Bro. Rinker possesses abilities which will make him a successful worker in the Gospel ministry.[6]

The recommendation was adopted at this October 23, 1885 session.

A second entry in the Ministerium's section of the minutes for the following day reads:

> On motion, President was directed to recommend a course of reading to Licentiate Rev. M. F. Rinker, with the understanding that he will be examined therein at the end of the year.[7]

This may suggest that Michael needed to continue gaining additional knowledge and/or skills in one or more of the areas outlined in Article IX, Section 7 above. If only the Hebrew language is excluded as a definite requirement for continued licensure, then he may have had some extensive studying before him at this point.

He applied for ordination prior to the 1886 Kansas Synod Convention in October. The positive approval of his application was given by the Kansas Synod Ministerium (as noted in the minutes of the Convention):

> As we find, after a personal examination (of Michael F. Rinker) for ordination, together with the evidence given (his) sermons and journals presented to the Commission, that (he) possesses the proper devotion of spirit, to the work, and the abilities which will make (him) a successful worker in the gospel ministry; therefore, Resolved, that ... Rev. M. F. Rinker be ordained by this Ministerium to the work of the ministry.[8]

Ordinations were scheduled in the middle of the Nineteenth Annual Convention on Sunday evening, October 17, 1886, at the Waterville Evangelical Lutheran Church (now St. Mark Lutheran) in Marshall County adjacent to

Washington County, where he would begin serving. Although those who were ordained at that time are not named, Joel Thoreson, who is the chief archivist at the ELCA Archives, believes that Pastor M. F. Rinker was ordained in 1886 by the Kansas Synod at that convention. Thus he became a frontier pastor. There is a statement in the obituary announcement made at the Thirty-ninth Annual Convention of the Synod of California, reprinted in that session's minutes: "Father Rinker, as he was called by his friends, was one of the first early missionaries sent out into the great middle west. . . ." His journey had begun. He was forty-five years old.

Four Churches

Washington County, slightly northwest of Emporia and on the border with Nebraska, was where Michael began his initial assignment as a licentiate. The area had not had a permanent white settler until 1858, when James McNulty brought his family from Iowa to settle in a cabin he had built. It was little more than twenty-eight years later when Michael began his ministry at a place named Greenleaf. The 1886 minutes of the Kansas Synod notes:

> In January, licentiate Rev. M. F. Rinker visited Greenleaf, of which pastorate he took charge by accepting a call in March. The reports of his ministry are very encouraging.[9]

In the 80th anniversary booklet of Trinity Evangelical Lutheran Church in Greenleaf, M. F. Rinker is listed as pastor from March 15, 1886, until November 6, 1887. By the time Michael came along in the ministry, a change had taken place in home mission work.

Up until 1870, each synod had done its own work in establishing new churches, according to Rev. R. A. White's *History of the Evangelical Lutheran Synod of Nebraska*. In 1869 at Washington, D.C., the General Synod created a Home Mission Board to bring together all home mission work under the aegis of this one guiding body. Each district synod transferred its home missions money to this board. Much of the work done by Michael henceforth, therefore, would have been sponsored by this Home Mission Board. The funding of the work in home missions came from several sources: regular offerings at the local church level, special appeals, and bequests from individuals with a commitment to this form of outreach.

This small town of Greenleaf had been laid out in November 1876. By September 1880 it had been incorporated as a third class city. It became a division site for the Central Branch of the Missouri Pacific Railroad (originally when it came through, the Junction City and Fort Kearney Railroad). It was named in honor of

Greenleaf, Kansas

the railroad's treasurer, A. W. Greenleaf. In May 1882, the English Lutherans had organized a church and were starting to build a facility for their activities. Michael was called to serve at Trinity Evangelical Lutheran Church in 1886.

By the time Michael arrived, the town had two hotels, five general stores, three hardware stores, two drug stores, a bakery, four restaurants, two lumber yards, two grain warehouses, a couple of blacksmith and wagon shops, a barber shop, two lawyers, and two doctors, according to William G. Cutler in his Kansas historical book. There were three churches including the one Michael served. Cutler goes on to say that "In May, 1882, the English Lutherans formed a flourishing church, and are now erecting a building."

Nearby, in Barnes, just a few miles east of Greenleaf, another church had gotten started in August 1879, named Messiah Evangelical Lutheran, along with a Methodist church. The Lutherans first began having their services in a store owned by Henry Ober, one of the earliest inhabitants at Barnes, according to Cutler; they later owned a building and shared it on alternate Sundays with the Methodists. No mention is made of this arrangement, however, in the 1907 Kansas Synod's history written by H. A. Ott. In 1887 the Greenleaf and Messiah Lutheran congregations joined to form a yoked parish.[10] Michael served them in their combined parish. According to the 1888 minutes of the Kansas Synod, Michael resigned the Greenleaf Charge on November 7, 1887.

He had been at Greenleaf for less than two years. The church at Barnes closed in 1906. During the years following Michael's pastorate at Barnes, from 1889 until 1903, six ministers served the church. Michael was not the only one serving brief pastorates.

On March 10, 1888, Michael moved on to St. Paul's Lutheran Church in Washington, Kansas, only a few miles northwest of Greenleaf.[11] Ott states that it was Michael who organized this church, but the 1888 minutes of the Synod

Washington, Kansas

Convention claim that it had been organized earlier, on December 11, 1887.[12] The congregation applied for admission into the Kansas Synod at the Twenty-first Annual Convention. He remained pastor at Washington until May 1, 1890.[13] According to Ott's *History of the Kansas Synod*, when Michael left the church was placed in a multiple charge with Greenleaf and Barnes, but the arrangement proved unsatisfactory, so it was discontinued.

Washington is the county seat of Washington County. Founded in the spring of 1860, by 1880 it was a community of nearly 1,000 people. Like Greenleaf, it was a town located on the railroad line, with all of its benefits and drawbacks. Actually two railroad lines ran through the town, for not only the Missouri Pacific came, but also the Chicago, Burlington, and Quincy Railroad. After the Civil War, in 1866, a large influx of settlers came through on their way west. Some remained and chose the area as their home. By May 1873 the town was incorporated as a third class city.

According to Ott, in May of 1890, Michael was called to serve St. Paul's Lutheran Church in Minneapolis (Long Island), Kansas, located in Ottawa County, which is southwest of Washington County. The 1890 synod minutes report that he was installed as pastor there June 8, 1890.[14] The minutes of the 1890 Annual Convention read: "Rev. Rinker resigned the church at Washington, May 1, 1890, and took charge of the church at Minneapolis." He was under the sponsorship of the Home Mission Board.[15]

It is worth noting at this point that these same minutes also note that Rev. F. D. Altman resigned St. Mark's, Emporia, April 15, and accepted a call from

Minneapolis, Kansas

the Children's Memorial, Kansas City.[16] Michael and his mentor undoubtedly remained in contact as they moved about.

Michael was given a letter of dismissal by the Kansas Synod to unite with the Evangelical Lutheran Synod of Virginia on July 22, 1891.[17] His leaving may have been related to Minerva's illness, which was cancer. He had officiated at a funeral in Kansas on January 2, 1891, so some time after that Michael and Minerva made the trip to the Shenandoah Valley. It may have been an opportunity for her to spend some time with her family. They remained there for about a year and then moved on again, this time to Indiana. The 1893 minutes of the Kansas Synod reported that the letter of dismissal to the Synod of Virginia was returned to the synod president, and another was issued to the Olive Branch Synod.[18]

Neither the Virginia Synod nor the Tennessee Synod, with which some of the Shenandoah Valley churches were aligned during this period of time, has any record of Michael serving anywhere within their jurisdiction. The *Lutheran Almanac and Yearbook* for 1891, however, notes that he served at Orkney Springs during that year, and the 1892 *Evangelical Lutheran Almanac* lists him as serving in Staunton, Virginia, that year as well. It is conceivable that he helped local churches by supplying their pulpits when their regular pastors could not. The Orkney Springs Parish at that time consisted of three Lutheran churches in the general area: Powder Springs at Orkney Springs, St. Paul's Lutheran at Jerome (about four and a half miles northeast of Bayse), and Morning Star at Hepner (about two and a half miles southeast of Orkney Springs). Congregations sometimes arranged with pastors to fill in as needed, with notification being sent along to the synod later. There is some evidence that some of Minerva's family may have been associated with the Orkney Springs church.

Notes in Passing

One of the major factors that contributed to the growth of towns in those areas where Michael served during this period was the rapid growth of the railroads. If a town came to be situated on a railroad line, it prospered. Those that did not fall on a railroad line were in danger of fading away or remaining inconsequential. The power and influence of the railroads cannot be overemphasized. In 1877, one line (Union Pacific) connected the Mississippi Valley with the Pacific Coast. By 1883, only six years later, three more lines were added: Northern Pacific, Southern Pacific, and the Santa Fe. By this time, too, railroads connected Chicago with the prairie and plains states, which meant additional market access for agricultural products. That, in turn, brought the possibility of access to foreign markets.

As America moved from being an agrarian economy to an industrial one following the Civil War, railroads became an immense influence in the way goods could be distributed. The growth that transpired was phenomenal. John F. Stover, in *American Railroads*, shares some statistics: Between 1865 (the close of the Civil War) and 1917 (the beginning of the First World War), the population of this country increased from 35,700,000 to 103,400,000. Most of these people were directly involved in the work of industry, either as workers or the families of workers. During this same period, the railroad network increased from 35,000 miles of track to 254,000 miles—a seven-fold increase! With the increase came power and the misuse of power until federal restrictions came into being.

What did this mean to the farmers Michael served? For one thing, it meant agricultural products could be measured for shipment not in terms of wagonloads, but freight car loads. The market expanded. The demands for their products increased. Not only were markets served more efficiently by railroads, but also people could travel with greater ease by boarding a passenger train. One wonders how much of the travel done by Michael over the coming years of his life was accomplished using trains. He traveled from the middle of the nation to the west coast eventually, not long after the turn of the century. By then, passenger trains were running regularly and carried increasing numbers of travelers.

Endnotes

[1] *Discipline of the Evangelical Lutheran Church*, 49.

[2] Roenigh, *Pioneer History of Kansas*, 2.

[3] Ott, *History of the Evangelical Lutheran Synod of Kansas*, 77.

[4] Eighteenth Annual Convention, Kansas Synod, 8.
[5] Constitution of Kansas Synod, 1887 Convention Minutes, 48ff.
[6] Minutes, Eighteenth Annual Convention, Kansas Synod, 32.
[7] Ibid., 33.
[8] Minutes, 1886 Convention, Kansas Synod, 31.
[9] Ibid., 8.
[10] Minutes, 1885 Convention, Kansas Synod, 6.
[11] Ott, *History of the Evangelical Lutheran Church of Kansas*, 210.
[12] Minutes 1888 Convention, Kansas Synod, 19.
[13] Ibid., 20.
[14] Minutes, 1890 Convention, Kansas Synod, 6.
[15] Ibid., 7.
[16] Ibid., 9.
[17] Minutes, 1891 Convention, Kansas Synod, 7.
[18] Minutes, 1893 Convention, Kansas Synod, 7.

CHAPTER ELEVEN

Eight Years–Three States
1892-1899

Indiana

Following his four or five years serving churches in Kansas and a year-long stay in the Shenandoah Valley, Michael and Minerva went to Indiana first and then to Ohio. From 1892 to 1893 they were in Indiana at two locations. In 1893 they relocated to Ohio, and after Minerva's death Michael remained there until 1897, serving in four places. From 1897 to 1898, he was back again in Indiana at three charges. His length of time in each place continued to follow what seems to have been a pattern established early on in his ministry—a short term.

Michael and Minerva came to the Richwoods Lutheran Church at Cross Roads, Indiana, on May 3, 1892. The Olive Branch Synod president reported

Richwoods Lutheran Church at Crossroads, Indiana

that "Rev. M. F. Rinker, supplying the Richwoods church, sent me his letter of dismissal from the Kansas Synod, May 3rd."[1]

The Lutheran Church at Crossroads was, at one time, called the Richwoods Church. The area was once known as Rich Woods because of the profusion of valuable timber there, notably black walnut trees. In his book, *The Trail of the Black Walnut*, G. Elmore Reaman explains that German settlers coming into this country and Canada looked especially for black walnut trees because they knew the land there would be particularly rich.[2] Nearby Fall Creek Township, with its Shenandoah High School, suggests that Virginians were among those early settlers in the area. It was in Fall Creek Township that Minerva was buried.

Some of Minerva's family had preceded her and Michael to Crossroads. Her uncle, Isaac, and his family had arrived there earlier. He was an elder at the Crossroads Lutheran Church. Isaac's sister, Rebecca, was Minerva's mother who died after her daughter, and she was buried next to daughter at Painter Cemetery. Isaac, who died in February 1884, and his wife Louisa, are both buried in the same cemetery.

This church is no longer active, though it is available for special uses thanks to the caring attention given to it by the Crossroads Lutheran Church Preservation Society. Located near the crossroads for which it is named—currently CR700S and 600W—it is situated in Salem Township, Henry County. Eventually the church became part of the Middletown Lutheran Parish. While serving the Crossroads congregation, Michael was probably also serving the New Castle church about fifteen miles southeast of the Crossroads community. Minutes of the Olive Branch Synod state that both churches were vacant because of Michael's reassignment to Beach City, Ohio. It should be noted that the 1893 almanac lists Michael as being at New Castle, Indiana. The almanac did not always agree with the convention minutes and, in every case, the minutes were the more accurate.

It is illustrative of the nature of the Civil War to cite some lines from Erich L. Ewald's article in the December 1996 issue of the *Indiana Magazine of History*: "Not one Cross Roads inhabitant escaped the war's fury. Candles burning by the window periodically announced to neighbors that one of their own had paid the price of preserving the Union. Despite the cost, loyalty to the old flag flowed unabated in Salem Township, a tiny corner of the Union that consisted of homegrown Hoosiers and transplanted Pennsylvanians and Ohioans. A large contingent of former Virginians, 188 of them to be exact, remained overwhelmingly loyal to their adopted state and the national cause."[3] There were Rinkers and Funkhousers among them. John H. Rinker, for example, son of Philip Rinker and cousin of Michael, was killed at Shiloh.

Ohio

Michael and Minerva left the Crossroads area in mid-September 1893 to begin serving one or more of the Beach City/Navarre/Sherman/St. James congregations in Ohio. East Ohio Synod records indicate he was to begin September 16, 1893. Their residence was at Beach City in Stark County. The 1895 minutes of the East Ohio Synod add this to the picture of his service in that area: "North Industry (about twenty-five to thirty miles northeast of Beach City) has had the benefit of the ministrations of Rev. M. F. Rinker of Beach City, for the greater part of the year. Navarre is being supplied, without the consent of the President for Synod, by a minister of the Joint Synod of Ohio."[4] The 1896 minutes note that the pastor then serving was attempting to take that congregation into the Joint Synod of Ohio. Apparently some usurping activity existed between the Joint Ohio Synod and the East Ohio Synod at that time.

This had to be a very difficult move for the Rinkers. Minerva was in the last weeks of her life at that point. She died at Beach City on October 31. Her body was returned by train to Middletown, Indiana, on November 2.

The funeral was held on November 4th at the Crossroads Lutheran Church at 10:00 a.m., and she was buried at the Painter Cemetery, located a mile and a half south of the church. The *Middletown News* published her obituary on November 10:

> Mrs. Minerva (Hamman) Rinker was born near Mt. Clifton, Shenandoah County, August 27, 1848, died at Beach City, Ohio, October 1893, aged 42 years, 2 months, and 4 days [sic]. She was the wife of Rev. M. F. Rinker with whom she lived in happy union for more than 25 years, 7 years of which time with her husband she spent in Mission labor in the west under the direction of the Board of Home Missions of the southern church (ed. Possibly the United Synod of the South). Her affliction was protracted and of painful character (being a cancer) but borne with patience and Christian resignation, and finally came to the end of suffering, so peacefully she fell asleep to be with Jesus; leaving a husband, a mother, one sister and a large circle of relatives and friends to mourn their loss. She joined the Church at the age of 19 and her greatest desire was to see the Kingdom of Christ prosper and His cause advanced, faithful to the end. Funeral services, largely attended, were conducted by Rev. P. J. Albright. The body was laid to rest in the Painter Cemetery to await the resurrection of the just.

Pastor Percy J. Albright was a Methodist minister who may have, on occasion, conducted worship services at New Castle and/or Richwoods because no pastor was serving them during this period. A card acknowledging the extensions of sympathy afforded the family by friends accompanied the article. It was signed by Michael, J. W. Jordan (Minerva's brother-in-law, husband of her sister, Fannie), and family.

Both the 1900 and 1901 editions of the *Lutheran Church Almanac* erroneously list Michael as the pastor of the Crossroads Lutheran Church in Indiana, and the 1892 edition lists him serving at Staunton, Virginia, church unspecified.

From 1893 until 1897, Michael was serving churches in Ohio. The fall 1895 minutes of the Sixtieth Annual Convention of the East Ohio Synod meeting list him at the Beach City Charge, which included four churches: Navarre Lutheran Church, Sherman Lutheran Church, St. James Lutheran Church at Cross Roads, and Beach City Lutheran Church.[5] Navarre is situated on the banks of the Tuscarawas River, northeast of Beach City about seven miles toward Massillon. In the 1830s, the Ohio and Erie Canal was a key transportation link; it passed through Navarre until 1913 when a flood caused a major disruption. Sherman was a few miles east of Beach City. Cross Roads was two or three miles slightly northwest of Beach City. At some point, Michael also supplied at the North Industry Lutheran Church that is located northeast of Navarre just below Canton. This is noted in the 1895 East Ohio Synod chart of assignments.

During 1896 and 1897, Michael served at the First English Lutheran Church in McComb (Hancock County) and Malinta's Trinity Lutheran Church (Henry County), both in Ohio. The Fiftieth Annual Convention reports of the Wittenberg Synod included mention of the receipt of Michael's dismissal letter from the East Ohio Synod to the Wittenberg Synod on January 16, 1896.[6] It was also noted that Michael had been installed at the McComb church on April 2, 1896. In just under four months, the following note was made in the minutes:

> On Sunday, August 30, 1896, the corner-stone of the First English Lutheran Church of Macomb was laid with appropriate services, conducted by the pastor, Rev. M. F. Rinker. The church is to be completed before winter.[7]

These are both in the northwestern section of Ohio, about 120 miles north of Springfield, where Michael and Minerva lived after moving west from Virginia. In their 75th anniversary publication of 1962, Trinity Lutheran Church at Malinta includes Michael among a short list of supply pastors who served from 1893 to 1901. The church was organized prior to 1887. His appearance in this list is unusual in that churches sometimes did not include supply pastors in their lists when they were making note of their pastors. The parochial report for that year provides the information that the McComb church had thirty-four confirmed members and at the Malinta church there were fifty-two.

An anniversary book put together at Malinta by Henry Geist includes some details about Michael's experiences there: "Bro. Rinker's services began February 1, 1896." It goes on to say, "The middle of May our pastor reports to the Synod about salary. May 24, 1896: We lack $19 of having our subscription full for Pastor. Received as Pastor's salary from members in amounts of: $1.50, $1.00, $1.00, $5.00, $1.00, $2.00, .50, $5.00, $8.00, $1.25, $5.00, .50, $2.00, $2.00." This glimpse into one of Michael's experiences offers another dimension of life at Malinta.

> Rev. Rinker and Henry Geist, Superintendent of the Sunday School, attended a Christian Endeavor Convention in Washington, D. C. the early part of July 1896. They left Malinta at 8 a.m. suntime, June 29 by train to Toledo, then by streetcar to the Pennsylvania Depot where they boarded the excursion train for the C. E. Convention. More "Endeavorers" got on at Tiffin and Mansfield. There was good "singing along the way, as they neared Canton they sang Sunshine in My Soul."

It seems clear that because he served for short periods of time as a supply pastor at several churches throughout his career, Michael was sometimes not included in church records, and few current members have ever heard of him as a former pastor of their church. This may be the reason for being unable to find him listed as pastor for any specific McComb church even though the minutes of the Fiftieth Annual Convention of the Wittenberg Synod note his installation as pastor at McComb on April 12, 1896.[8] His short terms of service are possibly one of the reasons why pictures of him have been very difficult to find.

Indiana Again

In 1897 Michael was back in Indiana. His location in the 1897 parochial report of the Olive Branch Synod was given as Broad Ripple, Indiana, now part of greater Indianapolis. While there he served Pleasant View Lutheran, East Salem Lutheran, and Ebenezer (Highlands) Lutheran Churches, all within an area now encompassed by Indianapolis. He was there, according to the 1897 Olive Branch Synod minutes, from August 1897 until November 14, 1897, as supply pastor.[9]

The Ebenezer Lutheran Church, actually the two churches with that name, had a history that included separation. According to a history written for the 130th anniversary of the Ebenezer Lutheran Church, the church was founded in 1844, and the congregation met in a barn owned by the pastor. Originally made up of a group of Lutherans who traveled from Maryland to Indiana by wagon and flatboat, it was located on the Millersville Road in Washington Township. In 1868 the church split into two groups called Lower Ebenezer (the original church) and Upper (Highland) Ebenezer (moved to another location) because of a disagreement among the members. The reason for the disagreement is not known with any degree of certainty. Some possibilities have been suggested: family politics within the church, the fact that some families lived away from the original church and nearer to where the second church got started. A language problem is not among the reasons suggested, because of the interest of the founding pastor, Abraham Reck, in using English in services. No mention is made in the history of Lower Ebenezer Church history of Michael F. Rinker as a pastor. The newly organized church coming from the division was later called the Ebenezer (Highlands) Lutheran Church. At some point in this same time period, Michael also served the Decatur congregation, possibly in Decatur Township nearby.

During this time, the Highland Church of this Ebenezer Charge was experiencing some difficulties while Michael was serving this charge as their supply pastor. The minutes of the Fiftieth Annual Convention of the Olive Branch Synod, in the president's report, offer some insight into the problems:

> On the 7th of October, 1897, the President visited Highland Church, of the Ebenezer Charge. A meeting was held, duly called, with this congregation, the councils of the other two churches belonging to this charge, and Rev. D. M. Horner, their former pastor. Some difficulties have existed of such a nature that do not really belong to the work of the Church, and should not affect it. One difficulty in the way to locate a pastor in the field, viz: some salary due to their former pastor, was removed, and the way is open to locate a man in the field permanently. Rev. Rinker has been supplying East Salem and Pleasant View congregations of this same charge by special permission. It is hoped that the field may be occupied very soon.[10]

The 1897 Olive Branch Synod minutes note that Michael served the Ebenezer (Highlands) Church at East Salem from about August 1897 until November 14, 1897.

In 1898, Michael was serving with the Rockport Charge that consisted of two churches: St. Mark's Lutheran in Grand View and Trinity Lutheran in Rockport. The centennial booklet published in 1953 by St. Mark's Lutheran Church also indicates that Michael was there as supply pastor from January 6, 1898, until July 17, 1898. Perhaps in today's terminology he would be considered an interim pastor; "supply" would suggest a shorter period of service. A few years prior to this pastorate, the church was named the First English Lutheran Church, but that was changed back to St. Mark's immediately following his service there.

Apparently Michael shared duties with another pastor, the Rev. C. L. Kuhlman, with one of them serving one church in the dual charge and the other the second church. In the synod president's report to the Olive Branch Synod, October 19-24, 1898, minutes, he wrote about this charge: "Rev. M. F. Rinker, who had been supplying the Ebenezer charge, closed his labors in the field November 14, 1898. By special arrangement with Rev. C. L. Kuhlman and the Grand View congregation, Rev. Rinker supplied the Grand View congregation from January 6, 1898 to July 17, 1898." It would seem that clarification was needed in the responsibilities of the two pastors and the obligations of the two churches toward them, for the president goes on:

> At the urgent request of Rev. C. L. Kuhlman, a visit (by the President) was made to Rockport and Grand View, January 20, 1898. We held meetings with the councils of both congregations, the object being to come to a better understanding as to division of services between Rockport and Grand View, and also as to the support of the pastor. On account of bad roads and high waters at this time, not as much could be accomplished as I had desired. The arrangement between Rev. Kuhlman and Rev. Rinker was sanctioned. The congregations are now, as far as I know, harmoniously cooperating with each other.[11]

Reading between the lines of the president's remarks, it would seem that there was a point at which the congregations were not living harmoniously, and perhaps the pastors were not relating to one another with a clear understanding of who was responsible for doing what. Or, as another possibility, it may have been that the one pastor (prior to Michael's coming) had not been satisfactorily serving two churches and so a "helper" was brought in to enable a resolution to the problem. In any case, Pastor Kuhlman resigned June 1 that same year, and Michael resigned a month and a half later, at the time the new pastor, W. L. Guard, began serving both churches in the charge.

Understanding what had been going on between the two congregations may shed light on this situation: Rockport and Grandview are about five and a half miles apart, located in the deep bend of the Ohio River, in southern Indiana's Spencer County, where it dips down toward Owensboro, Kentucky. Both were small river towns, less than one and a half square miles in size; in the surrounding area agricultural interests prevailed.

St. John's Evangelical Lutheran Church in Rockport had been organized in March 1870, but by October 1896 some members withdrew from St. John's to form Trinity Lutheran Church. The split took place because a group of St. John's members—where services were held in German—desired to have English services. Michael entered the picture shortly after Trinity was formed. The two churches, St. Mark's and Trinity, became a yoked charge on the north bank of the Ohio River, and pastors sometimes traveled between the two by river packets (steam boats). In the thirty-four years between 1859 and 1893, St. Mark's had seventeen different pastors. It is of interest to note that the two churches finally merged to form Holy Cross Lutheran Church in 1984, nearly a century after Michael had been serving there with Pastor Kuhlman.

Kentucky

From the Rockport Charge, Michael next went to Shepherdsville, Kentucky, where he served the Cedar Grove Mission, east of the town. The 1899 Olive Branch Synod minutes list him as supply pastor for this church.[12] The minutes of the 53rd Annual Convention of the Olive Branch Synod, a year later, provide some glimpses into how Michael was supported: "At the last meeting of the Synod a special fund was raised by private subscriptions to aid this congregation to the amount of ten dollars a month in support of a pastor, in case they could secure one. . . . Your committee has secured thus far sufficient money to authorize the Treasurer to make the payments that were due."[13] By 1935 this church had united with the Bethany Lutheran Church in Louisville, Kentucky. Shepherdsville is about twenty miles south of Louisville in Bullitt County.

One of the unique features of Michael's work at Shepherdsville is that it is the only church for which we have a report of the impressions of Michael while he was pastor. In the minutes of the Fifty-third Annual Convention of the Olive Branch Synod held in November 1900, we find the following:

> The congregation secured the services of Rev. Rinker as regular pastor. . . . The pastor reports the work of the year very satisfactory; increased interest manifested in the services of God's house; and also in the improvement of church property. Some of the young people seem to manifest quite an interest. Whilst there have been

no accessions made during the past year, yet the young people that are growing up are reported to make accessible material for the near future. Rev. Rinker feels himself to be compelled to lay down the work in this field at the close of the year on account of the much travel on horseback, which he cannot endure, but thinks that the field should not be left without a pastor.[14]

Michael was, by this time, nearly sixty years old. The 1900 federal census, however, has him listed as fifty years old, an error. He was living as a boarder with the George W. Lutes family at Leaches Precinct in Bullitt County. This family, in 1900, consisted of Mr. and Mrs. Lutes and their daughter, Mamie. Mr. Lutes, a farmer living at Salt River at the time of his death, was probably a member of the Cedar Grove church served by Michael, because when Mr. Lutes died in January of 1911 he was buried at the Cedar Grove cemetery according to the obituary appearing in *The Bullitt Pioneer* on January 6.

Cedar Grove Lutheran Church is illustrative of the kind of comings and goings to which small churches were subject. When Michael resigned at the end of 1900, the synod decided to yoke it with the Jeffersontown Charge made up of two churches, one having seventy and the other forty-five members respectively. The report of the Committee on Vacancies, in the Fifty-third Annual Convention minutes, reads: "That the Cedar Grove Church be supplied with preaching one Sunday in the month in connection with the Jeffersontown Charge."[15] This came about as a result of the request made by the Home Mission Board earlier: "That the Synod give definite instructions as to what should be done for Cedar Grove Mission at the close of the present pastoral year (when Michael resigned.)" The church itself cannot be found in that area now because in 1935 its remaining ten members merged with Bethany Lutheran Church in Louisville, according to the minutes of the Kentucky-Tennessee Synod for that year.

Notes in Passing

Bullitt County, Kentucky, was once a locale in which salt mining and mineral springs were prospering. When better methods for getting salt were developed shortly after the mid-nineteenth century, it was no longer profitable to go after the small quantities that remained in the area. The mineral springs still attracted visitors into the early twentieth century. The main occupation reverted again to agriculture.

By 1855 the Louisville and Nashville Railroad came through Shepherdsville, and the town prospered. Shepherdsville, where Michael served Cedar Grove Church at the turn of the century, had received a pounding as both sides came and went during the Civil War. Young men from the families there served with both the

Union forces and the Confederates. The area became a central point through which goods were shipped to the South from Louisville until it was stopped by the Union Army. It was possible for a steamer (packet) with a shallow draft to navigate as far as Shepherdsville to unload goods such as hay, timber, and livestock.

By the time Michael served in the area, it might be hoped that the wounds left by the war had started to heal. Reconciliation had begun, although memories might have slowed the process somewhat. Michael's efforts may have been part of the healing process as those of the generation who fought tried to resume normal lives in spite of those memories that lingered.

Endnotes

[1] Minutes, 1892 Convention, Olive Branch Synod, 45.
[2] Reamon, *Trail of the Black Walnut*, 65.
[3] *Indiana Magazine of History*, December 1996, 349.
[4] Minutes, 1895 Convention, East Ohio Synod, 42.
[5] Ibid., 42.
[6] Minutes, 1896 Convention, Wittenberg Synod, 10.
[7] Ibid., 10.
[8] Ibid., 10.
[9] Minutes, 1897 Convention, Olive Branch Synod, 10.
[10] Minutes, 1898 Convention, Olive Branch Synod, 9.
[11] Ibid., 9.
[12] Minutes, 1899 Convention, Olive Branch Synod, 8.
[13] Minutes, 1900 Convention, Olive Branch Synod, 17.
[14] Ibid., 17.
[15] Ibid., 18.

CHAPTER TWELVE

Three States in Six Years
1900-1905

Oklahoma

From 1900 through 1906, Michael extended his ministry into at least three states: Nebraska, Colorado, and back again to Kansas. They were all one- or two-year terms of service. In the 1902 *Lutheran Almanac*, Michael appeared as pastor at Blackwell, Oklahoma. In 1903, he was listed at Yutan, Nebraska. In 1905, he was at Canon City, Colorado, and in 1906, at Norcatur, Kansas.

According to a history written for North Central Oklahoma "Rooted in the Past Growing for the Future," Vol. II/NCOHA, St. John's Lutheran Church was established in or near Blackwell at least by 1901 when their first pastor was called. It is conceivable that Michael helped canvass the area to learn if a church would prosper there and organized it as he had done for other churches; he is not listed as one of the pastors. Oklahoma is south of Kansas and was at one time part of the Kansas Synod.

Nebraska

Yutan is located in eastern Nebraska. Originally named Clear Creek, it became Yutan in 1884 in memory of the Oto-Missouri Indian chief, Ietan. The town is located in Saunders County. When Michael was at Yutan, he was pastor of Zion Lutheran Church, according to a letter to an editor back in Virginia he sent in mid-January of 1902. In his letter he describes the town thus: "Yutan is on the Union Pacific Railroad. . . . Our town is three miles from the Platte River, a famous stream with much of romance about it. The climate here is fine, and the prairie is beautiful—rolling table land well adapted to farming. Large shipments of hogs, cattle, hay and general farm products are forwarded from Yutan to Omaha and other points."

This is the third of only four pieces of correspondence that have been found to be authored by Michael. Like the first from Spotsylvania Courthouse, this one is well-written and full of imagery.

The Yutan letter has no misspellings or grammatical errors. One would expect the training at Wittenberg to account for the improvement. The imbedded statistics are amazing and worthy of a Chamber of Commerce brochure. One would wonder if Michael was lonesome and trying to reach out to his old homeland. He was a widower, alone in a new town. He would not be staying there long enough to establish significant bonds. He may have written a lot of letters.

During part of his time in Nebraska (1902-1904), Michael also served a church at Roca, while also at Yutan. Yutan is located twenty-two miles west of Omaha; Roca is about twenty miles south of Lincoln, which means they were probably at least fifty miles apart. The minutes of the Thirtieth Annual Convention of the Nebraska Synod report that Michael resigned from the Roca church on June 1, 1902, because the Yutan church required all of his time.[1]

> **Nebraska Letter.**
>
> YUTAN, NEB., Jan. 22, 1902.
>
> MESSRS. EDITORS|: Some time has passed since you have heard from me, and no doubt your readers will be interested to read a line from this rich, fertile country of the far West.
>
> Many of my associates of boyhood days will remember me, as I am from the dear old Shenandoah Valley. I am now here where the great Platte flows on to the father of waters.
>
> Yutan is on the Union Pacific Railroad. This road has made wonderful improvements and expended hundreds of thousands of dollars in making a new line across the mountains, reducing the grade from 98 to 43.3 feet to the mile and crossing the Rocky Mountains 247 feet lower than formerly. Our town is three miles from the Platte river, a famous stream with much of romance about it. The climate here is fine, and the prairie is beautiful—rolling table land well adapted to farming. Large shipments of hogs, cattle, hay and general farm products are forwarded from Yutan to Omaha and other points. M. F. RINKER, *pastor* Zion Luth. Church.

Apparently Michael had written to the same newspaper at an earlier time, for he says in his letter, "Some time has passed since you have heard from me, and no doubt your readers will be interested to read a line from this rich, fertile country of the far West." He goes on to say, "Many of my associates of boyhood days will remember me, as I am from the dear old Shenandoah Valley."

A more objective appraisal of the climate at his new location may be found in the 1890 study done by the Senate Executive Committee, *Climate of Nebraska*, in which the report reads: "Winters of considerable severity, summers of unusual warmth, rainfall in limited quantities, marked and sudden changes in temperature."[2] The wind, too, could come howling across those plains at times.

When Michael was at Yutan, the population of Nebraska was 1,066,300 (1900). The growth of the state can be judged by the decades preceding that

98 | Michael F. Rinker: Pioneer Pastor

year: 1860—28,841; 1870—122,993; 1880—452,842; 1890—1,062,656. It had begun to decline soon after Michael reached Yutan. The population shift was caused by several factors. Some undoubtedly affected the people with whom Michael served. Nationally there was an effect generated by the hard times being experienced. The earlier land boom had resulted in seriously inflated land prices. A series of hard droughts plagued the area shortly before the turn of the century. Homes were abandoned, and the size of towns diminished.

The population makeup included 65,506 Germans; 24,693 Swedish, and 9,237 English foreign-born folk in 1900. Some responded to the presence of Lutheran churches, for 59,485 communicant members were counted. The Roman Catholic Church was present to the extent of 100,263 communicants; the Methodists had 64,352. Back then, 16.6 percent of Nebraska residents were foreign-born. There were, in addition, 43.3 percent from other states living there.[3]

By the time Michael reached Nebraska, the Native Americans had been subdued in large measure. Tribal lands had been confiscated except for small segments that were divided among tribes according to the usual governmental arbitrariness and unfairness. It is interesting to note that some Indians were taxed and others were not. Those who were not citizens, presumably, remained apart and, although they were the caretakers of the land before the settlers arrived, had little to say in determining the outcome of land usage or distribution. One wonders if any missionary activities had been carried out with these displaced natives. It would be noteworthy to learn what Michael's attitude was toward the Native Americans.

Zion Lutheran Church illustrates the kind of conflict that had become part of the Lutheran picture toward the end of the nineteenth century after years of accumulating problems involving language and tradition. Originally organized as an English Lutheran Church in 1882, the congregation began holding services in their new building in the summer of 1884. By the close of 1886 the communicant membership was twenty-four. They were able to carry on the work of the church without aid from the Home Mission Board. During the pastorates of the first two ministers, differences began to emerge among members of the congregation. Although the church had been organized as an English church, German families in the surrounding area had begun attending and gradually outnumbered the English-speaking segment. Services were often in both German and English.

The third pastor favored the German constituency according to one history of the church's life. The English members wanted him to leave, but the vote that was taken in September of 1899 was overwhelmingly in favor of his pastorate (120 to ten, largely on German/English lines) and appeared to be a mandate for him to remain. Dissatisfaction continued. On May 27, 1901, the German members of

Church and parsonage at Yutan, Nebraska

the congregation organized into a separate congregation and continued the Zion name. They became part of the German Evangelical Lutheran Synod of Nebraska. Michael's ministry at Zion, therefore, was primarily to the German congregation that remained after the split. His bilingual skills undoubtedly proved beneficial.

The English segment organized their own church as well on that same date and became St. John's Evangelical Lutheran Church. In their separation agreement, the property was divided so that St. John's received the church building and Zion received the parsonage, stable, and garden. Note of this is made in the 1904 synod minutes, when the president reported: "We have a noble people, though the congregation is small. The contest for the possession of the parsonage has been decided in favor of the German congregation. This is a serious blow for our people."[4] The German segment eventually became part of the German Synod of Nebraska. Shortly thereafter, Michael began serving Zion and seems to have remained there until July 5, 1904, at which time, according to the 1904 convention minutes, he "was dismissed to the Rocky Mountain Synod, where he is engaged in mission work."[5] He was listed in the minutes of the Fifty-fourth Annual Convention of the Olive Branch Synod as having his membership transferred on July 5, 1901, to the Nebraska Synod.

In his July 8, 1904 report to the Board of Home Missions in Baltimore, the Rev. Luther P. Ludden, field secretary for the Western District, shared this information:

> Since Pastor Rinker left them [Yutan], the English people have
> not been able to find a pastor who could serve them for the amount

they can raise. They gave Rev. Rinker $350 and the two rooms in the second story of the church. Synod asks if the Board cannot aid them with a small appropriation and let the missionary take up the work at Wahoo at least one half of his time be given to Wahoo which is but 12 miles away and has fairly good train service between the two towns. . . . we have the only English service in town. . . . There are two German churches, Lutheran and Reformed, and the young people of all the community come to our services in the evening.

This suggests that Michael was serving the English people (St. John's), but the records seem to indicate he served the German congregation (Zion). Since the German group retained the church building and Michael was given accommodations on the second floor of the church building, it seems clear he served not the English group for any extended length of time, but the Germans.

This provides us with some insights about Michael's work at Yutan. First, he seems to have attracted young people. Second, even though it sounds as though he served the English-speaking church at Yutan, perhaps for a time he served both. There remains some confusion about this. And third, while we do not know the period of time for which he was paid $350, the amount was insufficient to keep him there, because the field secretary realized that more would be needed for competent leadership. This fact of life for pastors of small churches probably recurred throughout Michael's ministry. Small, just-getting-started churches could not afford to pay very much. He would have had to struggle as best he could on what he earned until the point was reached at which he could no longer continue.

It is noteworthy that just about half (49.7 percent) of the current inhabitants of Yutan traced their ancestry back to one of the nationalities that would have been part of the early Lutheran churches, according to 2000 statistics. Of the four groups (German, Swedish, Norwegian, and Danish), the present German portion makes up about 42.4 percent of the town's population. Although the current church affiliations of these descendants are unknown, there are two churches in Yutan currently that might have some roots in their ancestors' religious history. One, St. John's Lutheran Church, goes back to Michael's time; the other, St. Peter's United Church of Christ, is within the historical parameters of the German Reformed Church tradition, and also traces its beginnings back to those early days.

Colorado

Cañon City, Colorado, is located about thirty miles west of Pueblo and about the same distance to the southwest of Colorado Springs, slightly south of the center of the state. Colorado is west of Kansas and at one time constituted another state that was part of the Kansas Synod. Fremont County, in which it is located, and Cañon City particularly, was the commercial center for miners who had come to the area at mid-century to prospect for gold during the Pikes Peak Gold Rush. Shortly after that time, when gold was also discovered at Cripple Creek in 1891, twenty miles to the north, ore smelters were built in Cañon City. By 1900, the county had a population of more than 15,000; ten years later it had grown to more than 18,000. About the same time gold was being found, oil was also discovered about six miles north of town, the first commercial oil well west of the Mississippi.

Michael is listed in the 1905 *Lutheran Almanac* as being at Cañon City.[6] The May 3-7, 1905, minutes of the Rocky Mountain Synod confirm him as being admitted on July 5, 1904, from the Nebraska Synod, and dismissed on February 6, 1905, to the Kansas Synod. With the influx of workers, the Lutherans undoubtedly saw an opportunity to serve. Trinity English Evangelical Lutheran Church began its life in 1897. The list of its pastors, however, does not include Michael. In his July 8, 1904, report to the Board of Home Missions in Baltimore, the Rev. Dr. Luther P. Ludden, the field secretary for the Western District of the board, wrote this about the Cañon City charge:

> Rev. Smith is taking a short vacation and at his own expense has Rev. Rinker supplying for him and at the same time Rev. Rinker will canvass the city of Florence. The city of Florence is in the great oil belt of Colorado a few miles east of Cañon City. Rev. Rizer made a partial canvass and found a number of Lutherans and at one time when I visited the place with him I supposed they would unite with the church at Cañon City and thus endeavor to hold them in touch with our church. Rev. Rinker will try and pick up the work and make a thorough canvass of the growing city.

By the time Michael became involved in the work at Trinity, a new building had been erected. About three years before he arrived, the congregation had purchased a lot near the corner of Ninth and Macon Streets for $850. By the end of March 1903, the building had been completed and was ready for dedication. The building, which had cost $4,300, had a seating capacity of 225, with space for related church activities. Cañon City offers a glimpse of two kinds of ministry performed by Michael during his years of service, both duplicated at other places over the years. The first was supply preaching in which he took the place of the church's pastor while the pastor was ill, on vacation, or taking a leave of absence. The second was community study, through which he could help determine whether or not there would be sufficient interest and support for a new Lutheran congregation.

Kansas Again

In the 1905 minutes of the Kansas Synod, Michael was received into the synod from the Rocky Mountain Synod on February 9, 1905.[7] He is listed in the same record as having accepted a call to serve as pastor for St. Mark's Lutheran Church in Norcatur, Kansas, on February 1, 1905. This church was founded in 1888, and ceased having services in 1984. Its structure has since become part of the Decatur County museum system and has been moved seventeen miles from its original site.

One facet of Michael's travel mode can be illustrated at this point. Getting from Colorado, when his ministerial standing and service were transferred from the Rocky Mountain Synod to the Kansas Synod, meant traveling approximately 330 miles by train from Colorado east to the general area in which Norcatur is located. In 1905 this trip would have probably involved the use of the Rock Island Railroad, which ran several passenger trains each day along the route. At prevailing speeds for trains, the trip would have taken about eight to nine hours. In those days, pastors rode at no charge in most cases. Throughout his ministry, Michael may have had opportunities to avail himself of railway transportation on many occasions.

The 1906 *Lutheran Almanac* lists Michael as still serving at Norcatur, Kansas, which is in Decatur County along the eastern border near Norton County. He was there from February 1, 1905, until April 1, 1906, according to the 1906 minutes.[8] His call to serve is noted in the 1905 minutes of the Kansas Synod; he was later received into the Kansas Synod from the Rocky Mountain Synod on February 9, 1905. The parochial report that year listed him as pastor, and the two churches that were included in that charge—St. Mark's at Norcatur, and St. Paul's, which was located at Long Island, about 25 miles northeast of Norcatur. According to the second volume of *Kansas: a Cyclopedia of State History*, edited by Frank W. Blackmar, Norcatur had a population of 482 in 1910.

While Michael was serving at Norcatur, he wrote a letter to a publication called *Record of Christian Work*, published in East Northfield, Massachusetts,

Three States in Six Years | 103

and edited by W. R. Moody. In the January 1906 issue, a portion of his remarks was printed: "I consider this magazine the ablest of the kind in print." It seems clear that Michael gained satisfaction from letter-writing.

Notes in Passing

During the last twenty years of Michael's ministry, 1893 to 1912, one of the major factors that affected the churches he served was the depression in America that began in 1893. Farmers in particular felt the problems associated with the declining economy; farm mortgages became unbearable because of declining crop profits. Foreclosures brought about family crises, and the church experienced the results of both the financial crises and the struggles of families trying to cope. Pastors, of course, experienced the crunch when church folk could no longer provide funds for the support of the church's work.

The causes of the depression that lasted for about three years included weather conditions—dry and hot during the summer—the resulting poor harvests, and the declining prices being received for wheat and other crops. Economic conditions in other parts of the country and instability within the government itself with regard to economic policies, were also major causes. Areas of western Kansas and Nebraska that at one time were thriving centers for agriculture, gradually saw their populations moving out. By 1893, the effect was exacerbated when farm exports declined seriously and private debt increased to unbearable levels. It was not until 1898 that conditions began changing; farm prices and farm export volumes began to steadily rise. Recovery was a slow process, and the lingering effects of the depression were felt for several years.

It would seem that Michael remained in the area through the worst of the depressed conditions. He was sixty-five years old when he left for the San Francisco area. Not exactly a time in life to make a new beginning perhaps! And yet he did leave. To what was he was responding? Perhaps an earthquake?

Endnotes

[1] Minutes, 1902 Convention, Nebraska Synod, 5.

[2] *Climate of Nebraska*, Doc. 115, Vol. 10, 51.

[3] *Encyclopedia Britannica*, 11th Edition, 1911, 327.

[4] Minutes, 1904 Convention, Nebraska Synod, 7.

[5] Ibid., 5.

[6] 1905 *Lutheran Almanac*, 82.

[7] Minutes, 1905 Convention, Kansas Synod, 7.

[8] Minutes, 1906 Convention, Kansas Synod, 8.

CHAPTER THIRTEEN

California
1906-1912

Between 1906 and his death in 1930, Michael served at least seven churches in California in one capacity or another—probably more if his supply preaching had been recorded. Michael was in California longer than in any other location except for his pre-war days in the Shenandoah Valley—twenty-four years. Although he "officially" retired as pastor in 1913, there can be little doubt that he continued serving in whatever ways he could as his health permitted, probably as a supply pastor to fill in wherever he was needed.

California had become part of the United States in 1848 when Mexico ceded the area in the Guadalupe Hidalgo Treaty. About six decades later Michael arrived. He went to California from Kansas in 1906. According to the 1911 edition of the *Encyclopedia Britannica*, there were 11,371 Lutherans in California at that time. Among the Christian groups, they ranked seventh. Both Germans and Swedes show up on lists of nationals arriving there. By the time Michael reached Los Angeles, the Santa Fe Railroad had already brought train travel west by way of its subsidiary, the California Southern Railroad; the final push from the east arrived there in 1885. In 1906 he was in Santa Clara, which is about ten miles west of San Jose and south of San FriscisCounty

San Francisco

Why did he initially go to California and, more precisely, the San Francisco area? Much of his ministry had been served in the Midwest, some of it in congregations that benefited from his ability to speak German. In April 1906 he completed his ministry at Norcatur, Kansas, after serving there for slightly more than a year. In 1906 he is included in the *Lutheran Almanac* in the northern California area at Santa Clara and Stockton. Orr, in his history of the Kansas Synod published in 1907, lists Michael in the brief biographical sketch: "M. F. Rinker, of Stockton, Cal." He is not listed in either record as a church pastor.

What brought him there? One possible answer can be found in what had transpired in that area less than two weeks following the time he had retired from Norcatur.

The devastating San Francisco earthquake hit that part of California in mid-April 1906. Churches were destroyed, and their congregations made homeless in some cases. The 1906 minutes of the California Synod[1] notes the following:

> St. Andrews Lutheran Church in San Francisco was totally destroyed by fire and the congregation was scattered; St. Matthew's Lutheran Church in the same city was totally destroyed by fire, 85% of the congregation lost their homes and possessions, and the pastor, too, lost everything. Other Lutheran churches experienced less damage, but serious none-the-less.

Could Michael have been asked to go to the scene to help however he could? No records have been found to indicate this to be true. It may be significant to note at this point that when Michael's dismissal record from Kansas arrived in California, it went not at the time of the earthquake but two years later in April 1908.

Los Angeles

Following his time in northern California, he moved south to Los Angeles and may have served at St. Mark's Lutheran Church while they awaited a full-time pastor. In January 1907, Rev. George R. Bird resigned as pastor there. His successor, Rev. J. W. Romich, began serving July 14, 1907. Michael may have filled in between the two.

In June of 1907, an obituary appearing in a local newspaper mentioned Michael as the officiating pastor for the funeral of one Ulrich Wanamaker. Mr. Wanamaker was a resident of Glendale. Which church was Michael serving at that time? He did not begin surveying the possibilities for a Glendale church until 1911. Does this mean that Mr. Wanamaker belonged to a church outside of Glendale? Perhaps the above-mentioned St. Mark's Lutheran Church? It was located south of central Los Angeles; Glendale is located in the northern part of the area.

A second possibility is that after Rev. Romich's resignation October 31, 1908, his successor, Rev. Jesse W. Ball, did not begin serving until December 1908. The home mission report for 1906 (minutes, page 23) says this about that charge: "In many respects this has been one of the hardest fields in this state to develop." The 1907 roll of the Kansas Synod lists Michael with his residence at Los Angeles.[2] The 1908 California Synod minutes note that he was admitted to the synod from the Kansas Synod on April 23, 1908; he had been dismissed from the Kansas Synod on April 18, 1908.[3] Is the length of time between actually leaving Kansas and being transferred to the California Synod an indication he originally had not intended to remain in California? When he got there and remained for nearly two years, his decision may have been to remain and not return to the Midwest. It was then, perhaps, that he requested that his dismissal from the Kansas Synod be sent. His intent may well have been just to remain in the San Francisco area as long as he could be of help in the crisis situation there.

The next reference to Michael comes when Michael would have been sixty-seven years old. In a report made by Rev. Luther P. Ludden, field secretary for the Western District, to the Home Missions Board, May 5, 1908,[4] in reference to a pastoral opening at a Pasadena church, he wrote:

> You will see by the enclosed "exhibit K" that the president of Synod was considering Rev. M. F. Rinker for this point. Never would do as the Board knows his method of work.

Exactly what this implies about Michael is open to conjecture. It may help to understand what is being suggested by considering the qualifications of the man Pastor Ludden recommended for the position. In describing him he relates such things as: ". . . may not be the greatest preacher in all of Pennsylvania, but he is a splendid pastor . . . young enough to be getting married . . . a good, faithful pastor, and that is what they need." Michael's age and the limitations because of it may have been the primary reason for the observation made by Pastor Ludden.

In his report of May 5, 1908, Pastor Ludden comments on the need for vigor in pastors.

> I am about of the opinion in our California field that the Board ought to change somewhat the policy in regard to men for these missions. I do not believe that the Board can afford to run a sort of a sanitarium. My observation is that in nearly every mission where we have a good strong man they show progress and where the man is sickly the work is sickly. I have an abundance of sympathy for my brethren who are not as strong as I am but let us be careful not to put men into the missions that need men who can get out and hustle.

Perhaps this offers a reflection on the condition of Michael in California. In 1908, he was sixty-seven years old. Maybe it also says something about Michael's motivation for going to the West Coast. Was it for health reasons? Perhaps he was among the "sickly" pastors about whom Pastor Ludden wrote.

Without intending to seem defensive, for Michael's ministry does not need defending, the reader is reminded of the times during his service that Michael was chosen to open mission fields and carry on the strenuous task of canvassing and recruiting members for new churches. He also maintained already established churches by contacting those who had been part of the fellowship as well as inviting new folks. It appears to be a reasonable assumption that in his later years Michael slowed down and could not keep up the pace required to initiate and nurture a new church start, or one that had faltered and needed new leadership capable of infusing energy and enthusiasm into the work. His subsequent work at La Crescenta, for example, speaks to his continuing commitment and ability to provide significant leadership. Similarly, his work at Glendale would seem to suggest that Michael was deemed to be a dependable missionary on whom the Home Missions staff placed considerable responsibility, Brother Ludden's opinions to the contrary notwithstanding.

There is currently a Trinity Evangelical Lutheran Church in Long Beach, California, that was organized February 24, 1907, with thirty-eight charter members. The first pastor, John M. Ziegler, resigned in October of that same year and the next full-time pastor, Daniel Snyder, came on the scene in April 1908. In February 1908, Michael was authorized to supply the pulpit at Long Beach "until the pastor should arrive," and his remuneration would be $5.00 per Sunday. He supplied that church for seven Sundays according to the Proceedings of the Eighteenth Annual Convention of the Synod of California.[5] There is no mention of his supply work there in the church's records. Long Beach is south of Los Angeles a short distance. He was living in Los Angeles (with a mailing address of General Delivery) at the time.

The 1909 California Synod minutes note that Michael did not attend the annual meeting of synod. His absence was excused; he sent a satisfactory reason for not being present. What that excuse may have been is open for conjecture. He would have been sixty-eight years old at that point and perhaps health issues were involved.

In the 1911 synod minutes he is listed as living at 1258 West Temple Street in Los Angeles. No pastorate is noted in the list of churches and pastors. Los Angeles was becoming a city. The population in 1880 had been 11,200. By 1890, after the railroad had started bringing settlers from the east, the population was 50,400. By the time Michael began his work at Glendale, the population of Los Angeles exceeded 320,000. When Michael died in 1930, more than a million people were living in Los Angeles.

There is one ELCA church in La Crescenta currently—Mt. Olive—and it does not go back to 1910 in its history. Michael is listed in the home mission reports at La Crescenta in 1910 and 1911. The 1910 entry under New Mission Fields states:

> Rev. M. F. Rinker is on mission duty at this place of 53 families (250 population), located about 12 miles northeast of Los Angeles. The town has a concrete church building, well adapted to religious needs, and owned by a man in Los Angeles. No other denomination is using it. There is no preaching point nearer than 3 miles. It would be well for Synod to consider this field at this session.[6]

Later in this meeting, $100 was voted for use at the La Crescenta mission. In the 1911 Home Mission Report, it was noted that Michael had conducted services at La Crescenta from January 16 to August 7, 1910, covering a territory of nearly twenty square miles, with very little remuneration. The report continues:

> Owing to the impossibility of securing a church property, Bro. Rinker retired from the field and the work was closed. For the same reason he declined to accept the aid voted by the Synod last year, and returned to the Treasurer of the Synod a check for $25.00, to which he was justly entitled. Your committee are of the opinion that this money should be repaid to Bro. Rinker.[7]

Synod concurred with the recommendation, and the money was repaid to Michael.

In 1911, the Home Missions Commission was charged with conducting a canvass of Glendale and the surrounding area. Michael was then seventy years old. This report was given:

> The Rev. M. F. Rinker was engaged to make this canvass, with the result that, on October 16, 1911, a Sunday School was organized and a week or two later a regular preaching service provided for. The Rev. M. F. Rinker has done faithful work for these people. On Sunday, July 7, they were organized into the First Evangelical Lutheran Church of Glendale. The congregation began with 26 Charter Members and an encouraging outlook. Rev. Rinker was elected pastor.[8]

A history of the Glendale church states that Michael led them through the organizational process at the I.O.O.F. Hall in Glendale on July 12, 1912. It goes on to say that their first buildings were built by July 15, 1917, a parsonage and a chapel.

The city continued to grow and expand, with significant milestones. For example, in 1892, oil was discovered there near the present site of Dodger Stadium. By 1923, the region was producing a quarter of the world's total oil supply. Water problems plagued the area early on as the need increased for a good supply. Eventually, the world's longest aqueduct was built, completed the year Michael retired from the Glendale parish. While he was in that city, Amy Semple McPherson's International Church of the Four Square Gospel achieved notoriety, as did its founder. Los Angeles had become a city where a variety of religious faces could be found, and the Lutheran church was in the midst of the growth and change.

Michael is listed as pastor in the 1912 synod minutes, where it is noted that he "entered upon his pastorate" at Glendale, September 1, 1912.[9] On November 7, 1912, he was installed as pastor, according to the 1913 minutes of the synod. The 1912 *Lutheran Almanac* listed his residence as Santa Cruz Street, Los Angeles; his residence, as noted in the 1913 minutes, was at 403 Bland Boulevard in Glendale. He retired from the active ministry because of health considerations in 1913. The 1913 minutes of the synod list his retirement date as August 31, 1913. This notation was included in the Home Mission Commission report:

> On account of a nervous breakdown, Brother Rinker requested to be relieved of the increasing demands of the congregation, and upon the expiration of his commission, August 31st, he retired from the work.[10]

One of the aspects of Michael's life about which we know nothing up to this point is his health. We might assume, because of his upbringing and his apparent ability to keep going throughout his ministry under what sometimes must have been challenging conditions, that he was robust and hearty. There has been no indication in anything found out about him to suppose otherwise. Only once,

---

FIRST LUTHERAN CHURCH MARKS 40TH ANNIVERSARY

With its campaign well under way to raise funds for a new building program, the First Lutheran Church is observing its 40th anniversary in Glendale this year, confident of erecting a new cathedral on East Colorado between Wing and Porter sometime this fall.

The history of the Glendale church really dates from October, 1911, when a Sunday School was organized at the home of Mrs. Frances Wanamaker near the corner of California and Adams. The following months the first preaching services were held at the I.O.O.F. Hall on West Broadway.

The congregation was officially organized July 7, 1912, with 25 charter members. The first pastor was Rev. M. F. Rinker, who served until Aug. 31, 1913, when he resigned because of ill health.

Rev. J. A. Flickinger was appointed by the Home Mission Committee and served as pastor until Jan. 1, 1914, when Rev. Gottfried Wenning was called to take over the pastorate.

He served for one year and on Feb. 21, 1915, was succeeded by Rev. R. W. Mottern. Dr. Mottern, now pastor emeritus, served until June 30, 1920, and was succeeded by Dr. H. C. Funk.

First Church Erected

At the time of Dr. Mottern's pastorate, the church was meeting in the I.O.O.F. Hall at Wilson and Isabel.

Under Dr. Mottern's leadership, the first church building was erected by the First Lutheran congregation on the northwest corner of Harvard and Maryland, with the first worship services in the new building on Easter Sunday, April 8, 1917.

Dr. Funk served as pastor until Dec. 1, 1928, and during his pastorate the present church building was erected at 233 South Kenwood.

Rev. Paul Luther Miller served as pastor from Sept. 15, 1929 to Oct. 20, 1936.

Beasom Becomes Pastor

Following Mr. Miller was Dr. James P. Beasom, and under his ministry the church grew in numbers from one of the smallest to the largest in the California Synod of the United Lutheran Church in America.

Dr. Beasom resigned Jan. 1, 1945, to become the first full-time president of the California Synod.

The present pastor, Rev. Carl V. Tambert, was called from St. Paul, Minn., and took over in July, 1945, and under his leadership the church has continued to grow and maintain its position as the first church of the synod. Mr. Tambert, now president of the Southern Conference of Synod has taken the lead in the building program for the new church. Last year the congregation voted to purchase the property on East Colorado, fronting one block on Wing to Porter.

With the completion of the funding program this spring, it is expected that the actual ground-breaking for the new church plant can be held in the fall. The present church buildings on South Kenwood will be sold when the new is completed.

---

110 | Michael F. Rinker: Pioneer Pastor

in the records, was he excused from attendance at an official gathering, and that might not have been for reasons of poor health.

"Nervous breakdown" is not a medical term. In the *Journal of Social History*, the spring 2000 issue, the authors (Barke, Fribush, and Stearns) suggest that the concept originated quite early in the twentieth century. They report: "The term became a standard part of American vocabulary, warning . . . of great psychological pain, of an impending clash between external forces and internal capacities." Michael was 71 at the time of his retirement. The stress of helping to bring together a new church, see to its functioning, and tend to the trials and tribulations of its members may have been too much for his wearied mind. The demands simply became too much for Michael's mind and body.

It may be noted here that under the leadership of Michael Rinker, the Glendale church, at the time of his resignation, averaged fourteen in morning attendance, eight for the evening service, twenty-one Sunday school participants, and nine at prayer meeting. A church lot was purchased for $1,150. Pledges toward the lot totaled $500.[11] We can be certain that his connection with this church did not cease when he resigned. We can be equally certain that his resignation did not come easily for him, but that his realistic appraisal of the needs of the church mitigated, in his own mind, for his resignation.

Notes in Passing

The city of Los Angeles had a phenomenal history of sudden growth when Michael was living there. In 1910, 19,964 people were foreign born, of whom 4,023 were Germans. In addition to this, more than 26,000 of those living there had foreign-born parents. A German language newspaper, among several foreign-language newspapers, was published. There was a significant German component to the society.

The urbanization of the city had developed with equal rapidity. By 1910 there were five systems of urban/suburban electric railways in operation in the city and its environs. Subways extended out from the city to its western boundaries. The 1911 edition of *Encyclopedia Britannica* (where the above figures can be found) describes the city in this way:

> The situation of the city between the mountains and the sea is attractive. The site of the business district is level, and its plan regular; the suburbs are laid out on hills. . . . There are excellent roads through the country. Los Angeles has beautiful shade tees and a wealth of semi-tropic vegetation. Towering eucalyptus, graceful pepper trees, tropic palms, rubber trees, giant bananas, yucca, and a

wonderful growth of roses, heliotrope, calla lilies in hedges, orange trees, jasmine, giant geraniums, and other flowers beautify the city throughout the year.

Such a contrast it must have seemed for Michael, coming from Kansas! And such a land of opportunity for those who came seeking their new life! It was in such a setting that the Lutheran church began planting seeds of faith. Michael was one of the planters.

Endnotes

[1] Minutes, 1906 Convention, California Synod, 10.
[2] 1907 Roll of Kansas Synod Pastors, 8.
[3] Minutes, 1908 Convention, Kansas Synod, 9.
[4] Ludden Report to Home Missions Board, May 5, 1908, 9.
[5] Minutes, 1908 Convention, California Synod, 14.
[6] Minutes, 1910 Convention, California Synod, 35.
[7] Minutes, 1911 Convention, California Synod, 22.
[8] Ibid., 23.
[9] Minutes, 1912 Convention, California Synod, 10.
[10] Minutes, 1913 Convention, California Synod, 26.
[11] Ibid., 26.

CHAPTER FOURTEEN

The Final Years
1913-1930

Retirement

The 1913-14 city directory for Glendale listed Michael living in the Flower Apartments upstairs over retail stores. They were located at the southwest corner of Brand and Broadway. The building is no longer there. He does not appear in Glendale directories prior to that. He seems to have decided to remain in the Glendale area for a while following his pastorate at the First Lutheran Church.

No census record has been found anywhere for Michael in 1910. In the 1920 census, Michael was sharing an apartment with Louis Hoffman, an eighty-six-year-old widower who had come from Germany to America in 1880. Louis could not read or write English, although the census form indicates he could speak it. At the time of this census, Michael would have been seventy-nine years old, retired for seven years since his pastorate at First Lutheran Church in Glendale. He was living with his friend at 1258 W. Temple Street in Los Angeles. Presently that site houses a bakery. Located between E. Edgeware and N. Bixel, the location now has the Hollywood freeway at its back door. The neighborhood would be between five and six miles southwest of Glendale.

Early in January 1915, at Glendale, California, where he then made his home, Michael F. Rinker received some mail from Virginia. It had been sent by the son of his sister, Elnora (Mrs. Joseph Foltz). The mail that Michael received was no ordinary bit of mail. It contained the very same letter that he had sent to his mother and father in 1864 while serving with the Confederate forces at Spotsylvania Courthouse during the battle there.

Michael's nephew, John H. Foltz, who would have been sixty-two years old when the letter was mailed, perhaps obtained the letter after his mother's death in 1903. Listen to the words John had written in one of the letter's margins:

> Will surprise you by sending this letter mouther had cept this letter many years I thought I woud send it to you it will remind you of home and war time.

How would Michael have reacted when he reread this nearly fifty-year-old message he had sent home to his parents when he was twenty-four years old? In the margin he wrote:

> Fifty years after this letter was written during the awful times of war the writer was permitted to read it through the kindness of my nephew, Mr. John H. Foltz. My nephew Mr. John H. Foltz of Liberty Furnace, Virginia, had this letter in his possession it having been carefully preserved by his mother who was my sister. He gave me the pleasure of reading this letter by sending it to me and on Saturday morning January 9 one day before my 74 birthday. write these lines.
>
> Michael F. Rinker

Was it intentionally sent as a birthday present? Maybe. Michael continues at another place in the margin:

> This letter is returned to my nephew Mr. John H. Foltz by registered mail on Monday, January 11, 1915. I desire that my nephew keep it.
>
> Michael F. Rinker, Glendale, California

John Foltz and his wife, Mary, lived in Madison (Shenandoah County) with their two children, Thomas and Cordilla Sarah. In 1910, John and his wife were still living there. In 1920, John was living with his daughter, Cordilla S. Sine, and her children in the same town, but Mary was no longer listed in the census. It would seem that Michael and his Virginia folk kept in touch.

During his retirement years, while he was still able to do limited service for churches, Michael may have shared in the lives of various Lutheran churches in the Los Angeles area. Prior to his death in 1930, there were at least five Lutheran churches in existence that are currently related to the Evangelical Lutheran Church in America: Angelica, Bethel, Messiah, St. Mark's, and Village. St. Mark's was one to which he may have related during the 1907 or 1908 period as supply pastor. He may have continued that relationship later in his life. There may have been other churches present that no longer are in existence.

In addition to the churches in Los Angeles, there were also two Lutheran churches in nearby Glendale, one of which (First Lutheran) he had helped organize. He may have retained a connection with this church in those closing years of his life. The other, Salem Lutheran, had come into existence a few years prior to his death. There can be no doubt that he maintained his relationship with the Lutheran church through one of the churches in the area, although we cannot be sure of which one.

During his time in Los Angeles County, churches attempted to keep pace with the growth as people streamed westward for varying reasons. The population makeup was changing as was the nature of the religious experience. In April 1906, the world was becoming aware of a new facet of the religious spectrum when Pentecostalism began receiving attention by way of its early (though not first) manifestations in Los Angeles. In 1923 the huge Angelus Temple was erected in Los Angeles as the headquarters for the rapidly popularized religion of Aimee Semple McPherson. Mainline denominations extended their influence by developing more and more local churches; Michael may have shared in this fervor by offering his services as needed and as he was able.

Journey's End

The Reverend Michael Franklin Rinker died on Monday, April 7, 1930, at 9:25 p.m., at the California Lutheran Hospital in Los Angeles, California. The attending physician, Dr. James H. Cryst, had initially seen him on February 27, 1930, so the critical stage of Michael's illness seems to have begun five weeks prior to his death. He was a bit more than eighty-nine years old. The cause of his death, as it appears on the death certificate, was chronic glomerulonephritis, a disease affecting the small blood vessels of the kidney that can lead to renal failure.

His life journey had begun about 2,600 miles away in the Great Valley of Virginia on a farm. His brothers had died before him: Nathaniel in 1896 and

Noah in 1897. Of his three sisters, only the death date for Elnora is known—1903. There had been no children born to his union with Minerva Hamman to succeed them. Their resting places were some 2,300 miles apart. The funeral service for Michael was held at the Little Church of the Flowers at 3:00 on Friday afternoon, April 11. His life is marked by a modest tombstone in Forest Lawn Cemetery, Lot 2664, Ground Space 4, in the Sunrise Slope Section. The cemetery is located in Glendale. On the tombstone is the inscription, taken from Philippians 1:21: For to me to live is Christ, and to die is gain.

Those who knew him in California had learned very little about his life. Apparently he talked little about his roots or career. Or perhaps those with whom he had shared his life experiences had preceded him in death. What was known about his comings and goings was included in the obituary that appeared in the May 8, 1930, issue of *The Lutheran*. The following is taken from that obituary.

> Rev. M. F. Rinker passed to his eternal rest after a few weeks' illness on April 8 in Los Angeles, Calif. On Friday afternoon, April 11, amidst a profusion of flowers and the presence of a number of his old acquaintances in the gospel ministry, in the "Little Church of the Flowers" in Forest Lawn Cemetery, Glendale, Calif., the body of "Father" Rinker was laid to rest.
>
> He had the honor of making the first canvass and doing pioneer work for Lutheran material in Glendale, Calif., in 1911 and 1912, and finally organized the present First Lutheran Church, July 7, 1912, with twenty-six charter members. He continued as pastor for a year; ill health forcing him to resign in 1913. A few years later he removed to Temple Street, in Los Angeles, where he lived in comparative quiet until April 1, 1930, when his weakened condition compelled him to go to the California Lutheran Hospital for care and treatment incident to his advanced years. On April 8, at the advanced age of eighty-nine, he answered the final call of his loving Master to come up higher.
>
> The funeral services were in charge of Rev. Dr. D. B. Huber, pastor of the Lutheran Church, at present holding services in the chapel of the hospital. Dr. Huber was assisted by a number of Lutheran clergymen of the Southern California Conference. Interment was made in Forest Lawn Cemetery.
>
> Mrs. Rinker preceded her husband to the Eternal City about twenty-five years ago. There never were any children to bless the

marriage. So the eighteen years and more he lived in Southern California he was comparatively alone, looked after by some staunch friends, grateful and true, living in Glendale and Los Angeles.

"Father" Rinker was one of the first early missionaries sent out into the great, little known middle west by the Home Mission Board. That was back in the 70s when the buffalo roamed at will over the Great Plains, and the wild Indian was everywhere on those frontier sections west of the Mississippi River.

After weeks and months of severe hardships in the eastern section of Nebraska, he succeeded in gathering together enough Lutheran people and friends to form a small congregation in the small village of Yutan. For want of a building in which to hold divine services during those early days, they were held on the open plains or in some woods nearby, when the weather permitted services at all. In that day when building material was very scarce, the first Lutheran congregation in Yutan had no little rejoicing when they dedicated their first "sod-house" church.

Having gone to Glendale in Southern California to spend the balance of his life, being a very active man, always keeping a "weather eye" open for his beloved Lutheran Church, he reported to Dr. H. L. Yarger, then western secretary, the opportunity he found in the small, growing town of Glendale for the organization and establishment of a Lutheran Church. Securing the interest of the western secretary of the Board of Home Missions and Church Extension, "Father" Rinker was encouraged to organize the present First English Lutheran Church of Glendale. In October 1912 when the California Synod met in St. Mark's Church, Los Angeles, the congregation was received into membership in the synod.

None of the friends of "Father" Rinker in Southern California knows where or when he was born or brought up; from what college or seminary he was a graduate; nor yet when it was.

He was a good man, keen, and farsighted, earnest, humble and self-sacrificing. He was clean in character, of a genial disposition, ambitious for God and the good of others. Kindness, charity and consideration for others he never lacked. He was a faithful friend, a loving, attentive pastor, and a good minister. His ideals were high, his methods thorough and painstaking. He had an unshakable and abounding faith and trust in the Holy Scriptures. With hope and joy he looked and hoped for the second coming of his blessed Lord. And in that most glorious faith he died.

In contrast, the obituary notice that appeared in the April 11 edition of the *Los Angeles Times*, Section II, page 1, makes note of his former service in Ohio and the fact that he left no relatives. He was living at 1258 Temple Street at the time of his death. No mention is made of his work in California, which seems strange, particularly the fact that he was the organizing pastor for the First Lutheran Church in Glendale. Either the reporter responsible for the obituary did not know where to find pertinent information about Michael or those of his acquaintance who knew him and were still around did not have the information to share with the writer.

Michael would not have been troubled by the lack of information known about him in those final reports of his life. Nor would he have ever insisted that more be acknowledged about him, his successes and sacrifices, his journey alone after the death of his beloved Minerva, or his comings and goings after his commitment to the service he had chosen. He knew that God knew.

CHAPTER FIFTEEN

In Retrospect

Michael was an ordained minister from October 1886 until his death in Los Angeles, April 1930, a total of not quite forty-four years, of which twenty-seven years or more were in active service. It would seem unreasonable to suppose that during his final eighteen years he served nowhere at all as a minister of the Gospel. Records do not reveal what his activities were in that period, but it is probably reasonable to assume there was some supply preaching along the way.

Michael's Many Hats

During those twenty-seven active years, he served at least twenty-four churches, sometimes singly and other times as individual congregations in a yoked charge. He served in various positions, including supply pastor, organizing pastor, interim pastor, facilitating pastor, and pastor.

Supply pastor: There were times when Michael simply filled in for an absent pastor of a church for a few Sundays when illness or some other indisposition prevented the regular pastor from being present. His duties would have been limited to preaching, administering the sacraments, and perhaps visiting the sick in emergencies.

Organizing (missionary) pastor: Sometimes Michael seems to have been the person, perhaps along with other people, who did the groundwork required for the organization of a new church start. His connection with the Home Mission Board would have been an indication of this kind of work. He went to the frontier, where churches were needed, to plant seeds that would later bear fruit. This may have been his most important work, if one kind of ministry may be given more importance than another.

Interim pastor: There were other times when a church was seeking a new pastor and needed someone to fill in for the interim period. His responsibilities might have included preaching, administering the sacraments, calling on members, officiating at weddings and funerals, possibly teaching in the church's educational program at the adult class level, meeting with the governing body of the church, i.e., church council, trustees, etc. Sometimes it might have meant mending wounds and bringing together folks who would rather not get together in conciliatory encounters.

Facilitating pastor: There seemed to have been situations when a church was in need of someone to help make a major change, such as merging with another church. This may have required more or less time depending on what would have been involved. There were instances, too, when a church closed shortly after Michael's pastorate. Perhaps the placement of him in that kind of situation was an attempt to serve the church, knowing that it would soon close. Some of these assignments or calls were supply pastorates and others, perhaps, interims.

Pastor: There were a few times when Michael was the pastor of the church he was serving in the fullest sense of that term. In addition to the responsibilities mentioned for the interim pastor's role, he would have been the church's representative in the activities of the wider community; the evangelist who sought to build up the membership of the church by regularly reaching out to the unchurched and instructing them according to the customary procedures for membership, creatively engaging church folks in reaching out to the community.

The fact is, quite clearly, those who were responsible for seeing to the pastoral needs of a local church—whether the synod or the local church itself acting independently of any other governing body—Michael seems to have been held in high regard, for he was continually involved somewhere in ministry. He went from one assignment to another, usually with little or no intermission. What he was doing, he was doing well.

The contrasts through which Michael lived are remarkable. War and peace, killing and healing, conflict and resolution, rural and city, alone and with a faithful partner. How much he had been involved in destructive acts during the war there is no way to know. He may have been entirely supportive as he drove his team and carried the wounded or imprisoned, or delivered the supplies that enabled others to carry on the business of war. Whether or not he bore arms against others is, likewise, unknown. That he was a healer is a certainty. Eventually, as he ministered in situations he could not have predicted when he entered the pastorate, he became a reconciler and healer among those whose lives had been torn apart and whose dreams had been shattered by conflicts and cultural differences.

On the Frontier

It should be kept in mind, as we appraise Michael's service, that he was, more often than not, on the frontier of this spreading new nation. He was called upon to take the church to places where it had never been, or to help sustain it in those places once it had been established. He planted the seeds that later would become strong, vibrant communities of faith in some cases. A few of his efforts did not result in the realization of a self-sustaining congregation; many did.

Not only was the nation undergoing growing pains; the Lutheran church itself was going through a process of maturing and refinement. This refinement came through hard struggles involving language differences, the nature of pastoral leadership and worship, as well as the outreach of the church into the world in which it found itself—not always in settings where the voice of the church was welcome, to be sure. That Michael was able to serve in these kinds of settings speaks well of who he was as a person of faith. None the less, there remains a bothersome question that needs consideration.

Studying the list of churches served by Michael, it soon becomes clear that he always pastored churches that would be considered small in terms of the number of confirmands making up their membership. Using the annual parochial reports published by the synods, the three largest churches he served in any capacity were First Lutheran at Crossroads, Indiana; Trinity English Lutheran at Canon City, Colorado; First English Lutheran at McComb, Ohio. The average number of confirmands for all churches served was thirty-seven.

Often, pastors of small congregations receive a call to successively larger churches. At times, average or below average pastors, in terms of their giftedness, advance only so far from smaller congregations to larger ones. Michael always served small congregations.

There are, of course, reasons why he remained with smaller congregations. It may have been so by his choice. He may have preferred working with small churches. That may have been at the heart of his service. That may have been the role in which he perceived himself as most effective. The churches Michael served had some qualities, in addition to their membership size, that mark them in distinctive ways. What types of churches did he pastor?

First, he organized churches where none had been. He started from scratch. He began with just a few and went on from there.

Second, he served yoked charges of more than one church. Usually churches join in this manner because individually they are too small to be able to afford a full-time pastor.

Third, he led established mission churches that had not prospered. Some of these eventually disappeared. His connection with the Home Mission Board sometimes led him in this direction.

Fourth, in at least two instances, he became the minister of churches that had come into existence because of a larger church that had experienced a split in its membership for one reason or another. The resulting splinter was small.

And fifth, when he chose to serve as a supply preacher for brief terms, he did so in smaller churches, almost—it would seem—as though it was an intentional interval between other places of service. How much of a choice he had in these instances we have no way of knowing.

There is another obvious reason why Michael served small churches. Few large churches existed in the areas where he served. He did not remain in any given position to nurture it into a larger size church. One other quality can be seen in some of his parishes that affected their size. They were often in rural settings, settings with which he was familiar because of his early years in the Shenandoah Valley. Back then, few rural congregations were large during their beginnings.

In addition to a consideration of the qualities of the churches he chose to serve, we would be remiss if we failed to consider the possible traits Michael himself possessed that might have affected his ministry in ways that caused frequent moves among smaller churches. This is highly speculative and very inconclusive at that. Very few comments about Michael—except for the obituary notices already shared—by others capable of objective observation have come to light.

Pastors can be caught in a difficult and frustrating position that parishioners sometimes fail to acknowledge. In Michael's day it was undoubtedly worse than it is now. A pastor who has felt called to serve God has experienced a very strong motivating pull toward service. At the same time, when a pastor receives such meager funding that his minimal personal needs cannot be met, he may wonder how much commitment that church has toward him while he struggles with them in their mission together for the gospel. There may have been times when Michael could no longer continue to serve a church for the simple reason that he could not survive the financial crunch it placed upon him. Some suggest that a man of God should serve without concern for the financial remuneration even when hardship persists. We might respond, a pastor still has to be able to care for himself and his family.

It is also significant to look at the Lutheran judicatory Michael was serving. The judicatory from time to time contributed funds so that Michael's ministry could be maintained. Before a local church is established, during preliminary canvassing and organizing, the judicatory would have borne the total cost of his upkeep while doing the work necessary.

Housing, Getting Around, and Finances

It may be appropriate, at this point, to consider a facet of Michael's life that is probably one of the "taken-for-granted" dimensions of day-to-day living. Mention has occasionally been made of where he roomed and boarded as he went from one parish to another. There would seem to have been three kinds of housing arrangements for him during his ministry.

The first, and one commonly taken for granted in our present time for some denominations, is the parsonage. In those churches that had been established long enough to have a church structure built, there may also have been time to build or buy a house to accommodate the pastor and his family. Frequently these parsonages would have been furnished, which meant that the pastor would not need to convey a lot of furniture and household equipment from place to place. The furniture provided would most likely be donations from church members out of their own homes of no longer needed items. Parsonages were usually adjacent to, or not far from, the church structure itself. The fact that Michael was alone during twenty of the twenty-seven years he was in active service would have enabled him to accept housing that would not have been appropriate or adequate for a married couple or family.

A second possibility, and one that existed often in churches without parsonages, was to room and board at the home of a church member. If the church was just becoming organized and without resources to fund the construction of a house for their pastor, then church members would volunteer quarters for their minister and his family. This occurred with Michael and the George W. Lutes family at Shepherdsville, Kentucky, while he was serving the Cedar Grove Church. Perhaps they started his day off with breakfast and concluded it with dinner; he might have been responsible for his own lunch. Or maybe other church members invited him to eat with them. This kind of housing would have been helpful to Michael immediately after the death of Minerva.

The third arrangement for housing involved the use of commercial housing, i.e., apartments or single rooms. This seems to have been the situation when Michael lived in Glendale and Los Angeles. The former took place when the church at Glendale was getting started; the latter occurred, possibly, while he was supply preaching at different locations. This mode was probably possible in cities and large towns more easily than in rural and small town settings. Obtaining meals depended on the availability of appliances and/or the proximity of restaurants. Living in commercial accommodations, of course, meant financial outlay that may not have been considered the responsibility of the church being served at the time. There was always the possibility of invitations to dine with church members when invited.

Getting from place to place varied depending on where Michael was located. In cities there may have been public transportation. In small towns or rural areas, as we have seen, horses were used to get around. At other spots, pack boats or trains may have entered the picture. Hitching rides with church members could have been possible. Horse and wagon mobility was in style back then, as were carriages. One would suspect that walking was a common method of moving about.

The nature of some of Michael's parishes suggests that he was required to do a lot of traveling to get to his parishioners, especially in yoked situations. At one point he found it necessary to resign from a parish because the horseback riding was taking its toll on his body. When he had to use public transportation, the cost may have been paid from his salary rather than from a travel fund provided by the church. Weather conditions certainly affected his transportation options. How many times he was called out at night to be at the bedside of a parishioner we can only imagine.

The records that have been found relating to him do not offer much help in trying to understand how he was reimbursed for his services. When he was at Shepherdsville, we are told in the Olive Branch Synod Minutes (Fifty-third Convention), a special fund was created for voluntary gifts to be used toward the ministry at Cedar Grove Lutheran Church. Ten dollars a month was given to the church by synod if they could find a pastor.

At Yutan, the church gave Michael $350 and two rooms on the second floor level of the church building. We don't know how long that was to compensate him for his service. He remained at the church for about three years, the longest period of time he stayed at any parish as pastor. It should be kept in mind that pastors may have supplemented their income each time they conducted a wedding, for example. There may have been other occasions in the life of the church and community for which they were also reimbursed.

When Michael supplied the Trinity Lutheran Church at Long Beach, California, he received $5.00 each Sunday. In that same state, while he was canvassing the La Crescenta area for a potential new church start, $100 was voted by the synod for that work, of which he returned at least $25.00 because he didn't think he had earned it. Whether that represented one installment of the whole amount he had received or all that he had been sent to date is unknown.

It would be remiss not to say something about retirement. When he resigned as pastor at the First Lutheran Church in Glendale, California, Michael was seventy-one years old. There was no mandatory retirement age, and pastors served as long as they were able. In 1835, the General Synod had begun planning for aid to pastors, their widows, and orphaned children. Synodical pastors' funds assisted those whose income from their churches did not meet their immediate living needs. Michael was helped in this way more than once during his ministry.

It is difficult to assess how adequate pensions were then. The fact that Michael was able to rent a room after his retirement may be some indication that a realistic amount was provided. It is probably accurate to suppose that he continued supply preaching as much as he could during his latter years. Such preaching would not carry with it the stress that full-time pastorates would, so he may have been able to serve in that way and, at the same time, supplement his income. It might be noted that he was hospitalized toward the end of his life, with five weeks of critical illness. How the medical expenses were covered is unknown. The hospital was a Lutheran institution, so perhaps there was a program that provided for pastors who needed financial assistance for medical expenses. Certainly whatever help could be provided was well earned.

Growing and Serving

Michael may have been well aware of his own limitations. There may have come a time, as he served a church, when he recognized that he had given them the best of what he had to offer and they needed someone else to carry on from there. Or he may have had an impatient spirit. When he felt they were not moving forward as well as he thought they should, he might have determined that they needed someone else who could better move them forward. Did he have a restless spirit? Perhaps so. None of this is to suggest he was not a committed clergyman. He was who he was, given to the calling he had heard back in Virginia, and fulfilling that commitment to the best of his ability. There can be little uncertainty in one thing: Michael went into situations that were difficult, from frontier to factionalism, from struggling clusters of folk to multiple, spread out congregations.

His life had begun in a pastoral setting in the beautiful Valley of the Shenandoah. It evolved into a pastoral calling, where he served his flock in many ways. An interesting sidelight: The term pastoral alludes to shepherding. Sometimes the one doing the pastoring has to get his or her charges to move in the proper direction. Sometimes they wish to do otherwise. Rescuing lost sheep comes with the territory.

The rural environment of a village named Mount Clifton was replaced finally by the clamor and melting pot that was Los Angeles. He had lived in at least nine states and possibly more. He had begun life with close ties to parents, brothers, and sisters. He had at his side, as he ventured forth beyond the familiar mountains that lined his valley, Minerva, his beloved companion. She had died too soon. He journeyed alone for the last thirty-seven years of his life. Although he undoubtedly had friends during those years as he traveled about, one wonders how closely attached he had become to anyone. In his obituary it is noteworthy that: "None of the friends of 'Father' Rinker in Southern California knows where or when he was born or brought up; from what college or seminary he was a graduate; nor yet when it was."

This lack of information on the part of his friends in California who were alive when he died may at first seem somewhat strange. It may suggest something about Michael's character. For one thing, he apparently did not talk about himself very much. His origins, his education, the range of his parishes over the years were not subjects about which he shared information, at least not with his friends in California. It raises a question about his own feelings about his background. Because he had not received a full education, perhaps in comparison with those with his friends, he may have felt at a disadvantage. Why would he have not spoken about his birthplace or his war experiences? Perhaps he had, but had outlived those with whom he was closest, those who had heard his story. Some had assumed he was a college and seminary graduate; that speaks highly of what he had become over the years.

Part of the answer may also be a result of his always-on-the-move ministry. The longest time period he remained in any given area, while serving churches, was three years, frequently less. Even while in California for his final twenty-four years, there were seven assignments prior to his retirement. By their nature they were brief. And when he finally retired, to what degree was he mobile? Was he often in the company of other ministers? Did they visit him regularly? What did they share in common with him? One would suspect that he would have been more interested in the church's growth and bringing people to God than he would have been in talking about himself.

The events in his life certainly affected who Michael became. His letter relates what impressed him about the war experiences. His reactions to his arrival back home following the war and the devastation he saw there must have left their mark. The deaths of his parents, Abraham and Rachel, happened soon after. His marriage to Minerva and her too early death after only a bit over twenty-five years of marriage, their inability to have children, their move away from all that was familiar to them, Minerva's bout with cancer and the frustration of being unable to do anything about it—any or all of these, depending on the individual, could be enough either to destroy one's faith or to strengthen it so that nothing would make it falter. For Michael, his life events clearly made him stronger and more faithful in his relationship with God. How did it impact his willingness to share of himself and his background with others?

Michael entered the ministry at a time when memories of killing and conflict were fresh, when places and people had been torn apart by conflicting standards of living. For some, greed had overcome a sense of social responsibility. Hatred for opposing ideals had ruptured the family of humankind in ways never before experienced in the new nation. Families and communities suffered losses that would forever scar their collective memories.

It would be difficult, impossible probably, to estimate the number of lives that Michael F. Rinker touched over the years in healing ways. Those who serve in pastoral roles locally reach out beyond their immediate constituency and come in contact with the larger community of which their church family is a part. He would have influenced many whose names never were added to the church roles. In many cases, he would never know how much of an influence he had been, perhaps in life-changing ways. Alone for many of the closing years of his life, he may have found this wider "family" supportive at times. As someone coming from the outside, he may have been better able to heal old wounds and bring together estranged individuals or groups. Having experienced most of the pains and sorrows common in those times, he could empathize with most to whom he ministered. He was known by some of his friends, when he reached California at least and possibly before then, as Father Rinker. Those with whom he had served, in those many local churches, had become part of his family. It may be that the memories of that wider family sustained him in his later years, as well as those of his life and family in the Shenandoah Valley.

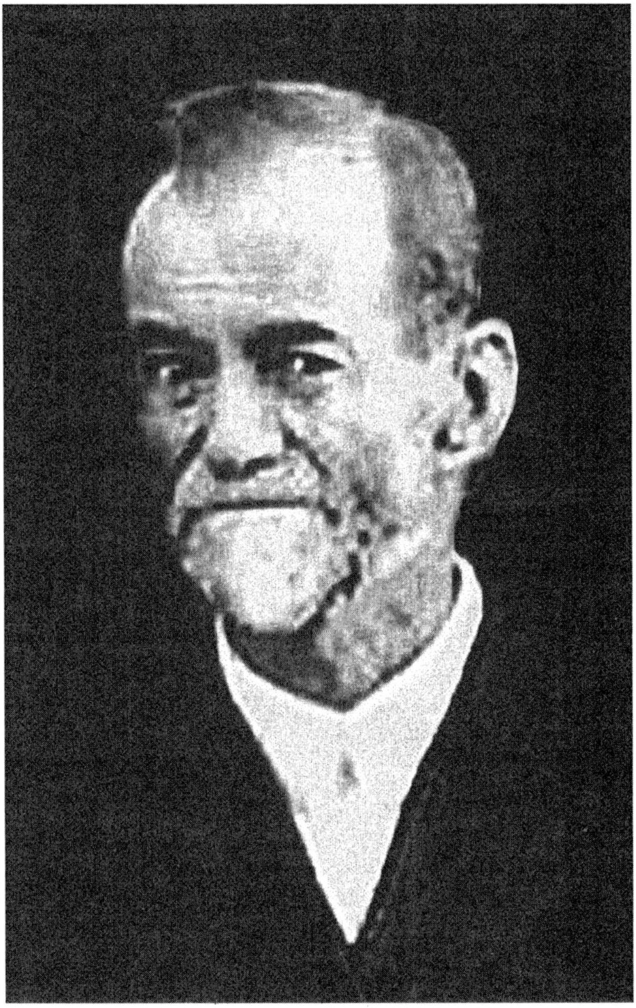

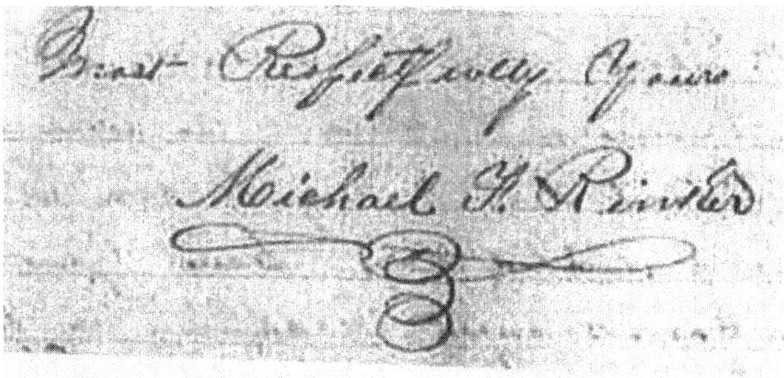
Most Respectfully Yours
Michael F. Rinker

Acknowledgments

The writing of history is not a solitary exercise. This book is no exception. Without some very special people it could never have been written. When we began searching for information about Michael Franklin Rinker, we contacted a lot of possible sources for help. Without exception, every one of them responded. Many shared what they knew; others were encouraging and suggested other places to look.

The discovery of the letter from Michael to his parents, at Virginia Military Institute in Lexington, Virginia, began the queries that would culminate in this book. Thanks to the efforts of the very helpful archivist there, we were able to obtain a copy. Our fascinating journey of discovery had begun!

Near the beginning of our search, it seemed to make good sense to visit the Archives of the Evangelical Lutheran Church in America located outside Chicago, Illinois at Elk Grove Village. We were assisted there by Joel Thoreson, Chief Archivist for Management, References, and Technology. This proved to be the wisest beginning we could have made. Joel explained what was available, made it accessible, and answered our questions. He was, and continued to be in the ensuing months, our best source of data. He patiently responded to our inquiries, provided copies of pertinent information, and made suggestions that led us to other helpful sources.

Two other individuals provided very significant help. At the ELCA Region Six Archives at Trinity Lutheran Seminary, in Columbus, Ohio, Jennifer Long provided assistance in locating data. At the ELCA Region Two Archives at Pacific Lutheran Theological Seminary at Berkeley, California, Carol Schmalenberger also provided help in finding information.

In addition to these three key people, other judicatory personnel sent material or offered suggestions of sources. Local church men and women shared bits and pieces of church history as they were able to find them. Some sent anniversary booklets or other historical writings, others sent notes about Michael's involvement in the life of their community. In a few cases, Michael failed to appear in any records they could locate, even though we were reasonably certain he had been there, however briefly.

One of the quests that proved most frustrating was the search for pictures of Michael. Apparently his picture was not taken very often. An initial picture came from an anniversary booklet shared by First Lutheran Church folk in Glendale, California. Unfortunately, it had been enlarged and used so much that it was not reproducible, but it did give us a glimpse of what Michael looked like, and this was to prove helpful when we found another picture. The second picture was one of three group pictures discovered by Carol Schmalenberger in Berkeley, California. Each of the three pictured people who attended a synod meeting in California. The picture for 1912 included Michael. He would have been about seventy-one years old when it was taken.

Local church historians, institutional archives, and local library archives also contributed to the total picture of Michael's life and work. Among the latter, special thanks are due to Jean Martin, archivist for the Shenandoah Public Library system, who invested personal time in scanning newspapers for items about Michael and his family, as well as finding information elsewhere that was pertinent to our project.

Our partnership in the writing of this book was a serendipitous arrangement. David B. Rinker visited sites connected to Michael's life, gathering pictures and information, seeking out references which provided the material out of which this book was written. He shared ideas of what might be included, suggested directions that might be effective, provided vital input as the refining process went on, and contributed some of the text material. Richard N. Rinker also gathered data from a multitude of folks and sources around the country. He took all that information about Michael and put it in order, then wrote the text for this book.

We are very appreciative of Leonard Flachman, Quill House Publishers, and his staff for enabling us to get *Michael F. Rinker: Pioneer Pastor* in print.

Both David and Richard are convinced that Michael was a very special and unique individual.

APPENDIX ONE

Bibliography

BOOKS

Burruss, Daniel Warrick. *The Rinkers of Virginia, Their Neighbors and Kin* (Stephens City: Commercial Press, 1993).

Cannan, John. *The Spotsylvania Campaign* (Conshohocken: Combined Publishing, 1997).

Catton, Bruce. *The Civil War* (New York, Fairfax Press, 1980).

Cutler, William G. History of the State of Kansas (Chicago: A. J. Andreas 1883).

Davis, Julia. *The Shenandoah* (New York: Farrar & Rinehart, 1945).

Defenderfer, C. R. Lutheranism At the Crossroads of America (1948).

Farwell, Bryon. *Stonewall: A Biography of General Thomas J. Jackson* (New York: W. W. Norton & County, 1993).

Heatwole, John L. *The Burning: Sheridan in the Shenandoah Valley* (Charlottesville, Virginia: Howell Press, 1998).

Hinman, Wilbur F. *Corporal Si Klegg and His Pard* (Cleveland: Williams Publishing County, 1887).

Hofstra, Warren. *The Planting of New Virginia: Settlement & Landscape in the Shenandoah Valley* (Baltimore: Johns Hopkins University Press, 2004).

Kercheval, Samuel. *A History of the Valley of Virginia* (Harrisonburg: C. J. Carrier, 1830/1850, 1986).

Kleese, Richard B. *Shenandoah Valley in the Civil War: The Turbulent Years* (Lynchburg: H. E. Howard, 1992).

Koons & Hofstra. *After the Backcountry: Rural Life in the Great Valley of Virginia 1800-1900* (Knoxville: University of Tennessee Press, 2000).

Lathrop & Griffing. *An Atlas of Page and Shenandoah Counties, Virginia* (Harrisonburg: Koontz, 1985).

McPherson, James M. *Battle Cry of Freedom* (New York: Oxford University Press, 1988).

Mitchell, Robert. *Commercialism & Frontier: Perspectives in the Early Shenandoah Valley* (Charlottesville: University of Virginia Press, 1977).

Nelson, E. Clifford. *The Lutherans in North America* (Philadelphia: Fortress Press, 1980).

Ott, H. A. *A History of the Evangelical Lutheran Synod of Kansas* (Kansas Synod, 1907).

Reaman, G. Elmore. *The Trail of the Black Walnut* (Toronto: McClelland & Stewart Ltd., 1957).

Roenigk, Adolph. *Pioneer History of Kansas*, transcription by L. Ann Bower (original manuscript, probably completed in 1923).

Steele, Alden P. *History of Clark County, Ohio* (Chicago: W. H. Beers & County, 1881).

Stover, John F. *American Railroads* (Chicago: University of Chicago Press, 1997).

W. August Suelflow. "Following the Frontier 1840-1873," *The Lutherans in North America* (Philadelphia: Fortress Press, 1980).

Wayland, John W. *The German Element of the Shenandoah Valley of Virginia* (Harrisonburg: C. J. Carrier, 1989).

Wayland, John W. *A History of Shenandoah County, Virginia* (Strasburg: Shenandoah Publishing House, 1927).

White, R. A. "History of the Nebraska Synod," *The History of Nebraska*, J. Sterling Morton and Albert Watkins (Lincoln, Nebraska: Western Publishing County, 1918).

Wust, Klaus. *The Virginia Germans* (Charlottesville: University Press of Virginia Press, 1969).

CHURCH PUBLICATIONS

Eighteenth Annual Convention Minutes, Evangelical Lutheran Synod of Kansas (1885).

Nineteenth Annual Convention Minutes, Evangelical Lutheran Synod of Kansas (1886).

Twenty-first Annual Convention Minutes, Evangelical Lutheran Synod of Kansas (1888).

Twenty-third Annual Convention Minutes, Evangelical Lutheran Synod of Kansas (1890).

Thirty-fourth Annual Convention Minutes, Evangelical Lutheran Synod of Kansas (1892).

Thirty-fifth Annual Convention Minutes, Evangelical Lutheran Synod of Kansas (1893).

Thirty-eighth Annual Convention Minutes, Evangelical Lutheran Synod of Kansas (1905).

Thirty-ninth Annual Convention Minutes, Evangelical Lutheran Synod of Kansas (1906).

Fortieth Annual Convention Minutes, Evangelical Lutheran Synod of Kansas (1907).

Forty-first Annual Convention Minutes, Evangelical Lutheran Synod of Kansas (1908).

Fifty-third Annual Convention Minutes, Olive Branch Synod (1900)).

Fifty-fourth Annual Convention Minutes, Olive Branch Synod (1901).

Sixtieth Annual Convention Minutes, East Ohio Synod (1895).

Fiftieth Annual Convention Minutes, Wittenberg Synod (1896).

Eighteenth Annual Convention Minutes, Synod of California (1908).

Twentieth Annual Convention Minutes, Synod of California (1910).

Twenty-first Annual Convention Minutes, Synod of California (1911).

Twenty-second Annual Convention Minutes, Synod of California (1912).

Twenty-third Annual Convention Minutes, Synod of California (1913).

Lutheran Almanac (Philadelphia, 1887).

Lutheran Almanac (Philadelphia, 1890).

Lutheran Almanac (Philadelphia, 1891).

Lutheran Almanac (Philadelphia, 1892).

Lutheran Almanac (Philadelphia, 1893).

Lutheran Almanac (Philadelphia, 1896).

Lutheran Almanac (Philadelphia, 1899).

Lutheran Almanac (Philadelphia, 1900).

Lutheran Almanac (Philadelphia, 1901).

Lutheran Almanac (Philadelphia, 1902).

Lutheran Almanac (Philadelphia, 1903).

Lutheran Almanac (Philadelphia, 1905).

Lutheran Almanac (Philadelphia, 1906).

Lutheran Almanac (Philadelphia, 1907).

APPENDIX TWO

Michael F. Rinker Family Line

1   Hans Jakob Ringger, b: 24 September 1724 in Nuerensdorf, CH d: 26 August 1797 in Conicville, Virginia
    + Anna Maria Nessen b: 29 March 1748 in New Hanover, Pennsylvania

2   Jacob Rinker, b: 28 March 1749 in Pennsylvania, d: 18 January 1827 in Woodstock, Virginia

2   George Rinker, b: 01 September 1751 in Pennsylvania, d: 11 December 1835 in Indiana
    + Mary Magdalene Surber b: 22 June 1773 in Shenandoah County, Virginia, d: 23 July 1839, Father: Jacob Surber, Mother: Catherine

    3   Joseph Rinker, b: 06 July 1800 in Shenandoah County, Virginia, d: 11 October 1855 in Lawrence County, Missouri

    3   Jefferson Rinker, b: About 1802 in Greene County, Tennessee

    3   Washington Rinker, b: 1805 in Greene County, Tennessee, d: in Aurora, Misouri

    3   Sarah (Sally) Rinker, b: 07 March 1806 in Greene County, Tennessee, d: 07 February 1876 in Boone County, Iowa.

    3   Lydia Rinker, b: 1812 in Greene County, Tennessee, d: 02 June 1877 in Madrid, Iowa
    + Catherine Negley, m: 28 February 1771

    3   Mary Magdalene Rinker, b: 1773 in Shenandoah County, Virgania

    3   George Rinker, b: 1776 in Shenandoah County, Virginia, d: 03 March 1843 in Henry County, Indiana

    3   Henry Rinker, b: 1777 in Shenandoah County, Virginia, d: 13 January 1834 in Shenandoah County, Virginia
        + Dorothy Dellinger d: 08 June 1833 in Shenandoah County, Virginia, m: 23 August 1798 in Shenandoah County, Virginia, Father: Christian Dellinger

        4   Catherine Rinker, b: 30 November 1799 in Shenandoah County, Virginia

        4   Absalom Rinker, b: 30 January 1801 in Shenandoah County, Virginia, d: 07 March 1869
            + Rachel Neese, b: About 1797, d: in Shenandoah County, Virginia, m: 26 September 1822

       5   Elenora Rinker, b: 21 February 1824 in Shenandoah County, Virginia, d: 14 December 1903
       5   Hannah Rinker, b: 20 Mar 1827 in Shenandoah County, Virginia
       5   Nathanael B. F. Rinker, b: 20 November 1828 in Shenandoah County, Virginia. d: 22 October 1896
       5   Sarah Rinker, b: 20 May 1830
       5   Noah Franklin Rinker, b: 14 February 1835 in Shenandoah County, Virginia, d: 14 January 1897 in Shenandoah County, Virginia
       5   Michael Franklin Rinker, b: 10 Jan 1841 in Shenandoah County, Virginia, d: 07 April 1930 in Los Angeles, California
+ Sarah J. Sell, b: About 1832, m: 04 August 1867, Father: Andrick Sell, Mother: Rebecca
       5   Benjamin Ira Rinker, b: 17 December 1867, d: 21 August 1937 in Manassas, Virginia

    4   Barbara Rinker, b: 12 June 1802 in Shenandoah County, Virginia
    4   Benjamin Rinker, b: 12 October 1805 in Shenandoah County, Virginia, d: 23 November 1880 in Northampton, Ohio
+ Mary Eavy, m: 13 October 1816 in Shenandoah County, Virginia, Father: Peter Eavy

    4   Washington Rinker, b: 16 February 1818 in Shenandoah County, Virginia
    4   Sarah Rinker, b: 30 November 1820
    4   Israel Rinker, b: 14 February 1822, d: 17 February 1884
    4   Christina Rinker, b: 18 November 1823
    4   Jacob Henry Rinker, b: About 1825

 3   Jacob Rinker, b: 1779 in Shenandoah County, Virginia
 3   Anna Catherine Rinker, b: 1781 in Shenandoah County, Virginia, d: About 1850
 3   Philip Rinker, b: 19 November 1785 in Shenandoah County, Virginia, d: 09 July 1840 in Carroll County, Indiana

 3   Elizabeth Rinker, b: 1788 in Shenandoah County, Virginia, d: 1840
2   Johannes Rinker, b: 24 March 1753
2   Elizabeth Rinker, b: 14 March 1755
2   Henrich Rinker, b: 09 January 1757 in Pennsylvania, d: 10 May 1805 in Shenandoah County, Virginia

Descendants of Christian Funkhouser

1   Christian Funkhouser, b: 24 July 1802, d: 26 April 1884 in Bayse, Virginia
+ Polly Painter, m: 24 March 1823

   2   Rebecca Funkhouser, b: 1816, d: 1898
+ Reuben Hammon, b: 02 May 1813, d: 23 October 1854, m: 26 Oct 1842, Father: George Hammon, Mother: Lydia Painter

      3   Minerva Hammon, b: 27 August 1848 in Shenandoah County, Virginia, d: 31 October 1893, in Beach City, Ohio

      + Michael Franklin Rinker, b: 10 January 1841 in Shenandoah County, Virginia, d: 07 April 1930 in Los Angeles, California, m: 26 March 1868 in Shenandoah County, Virginia, Father: Absalom Rinker, Mother: Rachel Neese

3   Mary C. Hammon, b: May 1842, d: November 1876
+ William P. Dellinger, b: 30 June 1839 in Shenandoah County, Virginia, d:1923, m: 1865

    4   Minnie Lee Dellinger, b: 30 July 1867
+ Samuel B. Hepner, m: 1885

3   Barbara Hammon, b: 30 January 1846, d: 29 July 1854

3   George M. Hammon, b: About 1850
+ Mollie C. Hudson, m: 15 March 1871

3   Fannie Hammon, b: May 1851
+ John W. Jordan

    4   Rudy Jordan

    4   Joseph Jordan

3   Alice Hammon, b: 27 March 1855, d: 15 December 1882
+ Richard C. Clark, m: 18 August 1874

    4   Bertha J. Clark, b: 27 February 1875
+ Robert D. Pence, m: 25 May 1897

2   Isaac Funkhouser, b: 27 August 1821 in Shenandoah County, Virginia, d: 15 February 1884 in Middletown, Indiana
+ Louisa Blose, m: 11 February 1849 in Champaign County, Ohio

2   William Funkhouser

APPENDIX THREE

Rinkers in Ohio Prior to 1900
(within 50 miles of Springfield)

1830 Census
Springfield (Clark County)
Joseph 30-40: wife and 3 children

1840 Census
Springfield (Clark County)
Joseph 30-40: wife and 3 children

Concord (Champaign County)
Henry 30-40 wife, 3 children

1850 Census
German (Clark County)
Benjamin 48 Virginia
Susan 44 Virginia
Melinda 22 Virginia
John 20 Virginia
George 18 Virginia
Anna 16 Virginia
Caroline 12 Virginia
Caty 11 Virginia

Springfield (Clark County)
Elizabeth 46 Maryland
Peter 25 Virginia
Elizabeth 16 Ohio

1860 Census
Pike (Clark County)
George 27 Ohio
Sarah 25 Virginia
Ann E. 5 Virginia
John B. 1 Virginia

Springfield (Clark County)
Peter 35 Virginia
Catharine 29 Ohio
Joseph 2 Ohio

Elizabeth 55 Maryland
Elizabeth 26 Ohio

German (Clark County)
Benjamin 54 Virginia
Susan 52 Virginia
Anne 24 Virginia
Caroline 21 Virginia
John 30 Virginia
Delila 23 Ohio

1870 Census
Mad River (Champaign County)
William T. 23 Virginia

Springfield (Clark County)
Peter 41 Virginia
Catharine 46 Ohio
Joseph 12 Ohio
John 9 Ohio
Charles 6 Ohio
George 1 Ohio

Elizabeth 68 Maryland

German (Clark County)
Benjamin 63 Virginia
Susan 62 Ohio
Anne 40 Virginia

Pike (Clark County)
Delilah 33 Ohio

1880 Census

Mad River (Champaign County)
Nathanael 37 Virginia
Victoria 30 Virginia
Cora L. 13 Virginia
Oscar 11 Virginia
Annie 8 Virginia
James E. 5 Virginia
Mary E. 1 Virginia

German (Clark County)
Benjamin 75 Virginia
Susanne 72 Virginia
Anne 40 Virginia

Pike (Clark County)
George 48 Virginia
Sarah 49 Virginia
William B. 16 Ohio

Springfield (Clark County)
Peter 55 Virginia
Catharine 44 Ohio
Joseph 21 (Ohio)
John 19 (Ohio)
Charles 16 Ohio
George 10 Ohio
Emma E. 7
Harry 6

Elizabeth 68 Maryland

Michael F. 35 Virginia
Minerva 31 Virginia

(The 1890 Federal Census does not exist.)

1900 Census

Pike (Clark County)
George 5.1832 Virginia
Louisa 1.1864 Ohio
Harry A. 6.1885 Ohio

Springfield (Clark County)
Harry E. 4.1875 Ohio
Alma R. 5.1877 Ohio
Frank O. 1.1899 Ohio
Catharine 2.1834 Ohio
John E. 10.1861 Ohio
George 12.1870 OH
Jessie D. 6.1877 [D-I-L]
Horace A. 12.1899 [G-S]

Union (Union County)
Elizabeth C. 6.1838 Virginia
Clara L. 1.1879 Virginia

APPENDIX FOUR

References to Michael F. Rinker in Lutheran Publications

SYNOD MINUTES

Synod of Kansas, Eighteenth Annual Convention Minutes (1885)

President's Report, Calls Accepted (p. 8): Rev. F. D. Altman, by appointment of the Board of Home Missions, assumed charge of the Emporia mission, May 26, 1885.

President's Report, New Organizations (p. 8): Rev. F. D. Altman organized the Emporia mission in June last with twenty-two members.

Ministerium, Executive Committee Report (p. 32f): There have been placed in our hands two manuscripts by Mr. M. F. Rinker, of Emporia, Kansas, to illustrate his method of handling the Word of God for the edification of souls. We have also had a colloquium with Bro. Rinker, with a view to his licensure. We recommend that he be licensed for one year, believing that Bro. Rinker possesses abilities which will make him a successful worker in the Gospel ministry.... (The) President was directed to recommend a course of reading to licentiate Rev. M. F. Rinker, with the understanding that he will be examined therein at the end of the year.

Synod of Kansas, Nineteenth Annual Convention Minutes (1886)

President's Report, Calls Accepted (p. 8): In January, licentiate Rev. M. F. Rinker visited Greenleaf, of which pastorate he took charge by accepting a call in March. The reports of his ministry are very encouraging.

Ministerium, Report of Examining Committee (p. 31): Your committee would report that the following persons . . . M. F. Rinker . . . have applied for ordination to the Gospel ministry. As we find, after a personal examination of these applicants for ordination, together with the evidence given in their sermons and journals presented to the committee, that they possess the proper devotion of spirit, to the work, and the abilities which will make them successful workers in the Gospel ministry; therefore, Resolved, that . . . M. F. Rinker . . . be ordained by this Ministerium to the work of the ministry. [An ordination service was scheduled for October 17, 1886 during that Convention.]

Apportionment Table (p. 34): M. F. Rinker, 36 members

Parochial Report (p. 36): M. F. Rinker, Greenleaf and Barnes (36 members, $7,500 property value, $131 local expenses for all objects).

Synod of Kansas, Twentieth Annual Convention Minutes (1887)

Clerical Roll (p. 7) Rev. M. F. Rinker, Greenleaf, Kansas

Synodical Statistics (p. 34): Greenleaf and Barnes, M. F. Rinker (69 members)

Parochial Report (p. 36): M. F. Rinker, Greenleaf listing Trinity and Messiah churches (19/50, $1,00/$1,500, $266/265)

(includes requirements for licensure and ordination)

Synod of Kansas, Twenty-first Annual Convention Minutes (1888)

President's Report, Pastoral Changes (p. 8): Rev. M. F. Rinker resigned the Greenleaf Charge, Nov. 7, 1887. Rev. M. F. Rinker accepted a call to the newly-organized church at Washington, March 10, 1888.

President's Report, Organizations (p. 9): Rev. M. F. Rinker reported the organization of St. Paul's Evangelical Church at Washington, and that it would apply for admission into the Kansas Synod at this convention, March 10, 1888.

Committee on Admission of Churches (p. 19): (St. Paul's Evangelical Lutheran Church of Washington, Kansas) applies for admission to Synod. This congregation was organized December 11, 1887 with 33 organizing members. The application is signed by Rev. M. F. Rinker, Chairman of the Church Council … The Committee would recommend that this congregation be received and enrolled as an integral part of this Synod.

Parochial Report (p. 42): M. F. Rinker, Washington St. Paul's (42,$925, $808).

Synod of Kansas, Twenty-second Annual Convention Minutes (1889)

Synodical Roll (p. 8): Rev. M. F. Rinker, Washington, Kansas

Parochial Report (p. 48): M. F. Rinker, Washington, St. Paul's (46, $925, $560.35)

Synod of Kansas, Twenty-third Annual Convention Minutes (1890)

Synodical Roll (p. 6): M. F. Rinker, Minneapolis, Kansas.

President's Report, Resignations (p. 7): Rev. M. F. Rinker resigned the church at Washington, May 1, 1890, and took charge of the church at Minneapolis.

President's Report, Installations (p. 7): Rev. M. F. Rinker was installed as pastor at Minneapolis, June 8, 1890.

Synod of Kansas, Thirty-fourth Annual Convention Minutes, (1891)

President's Report (p. 7): July 22, 1891, Rev. M. F. Rinker was given a letter to unite with the Evangelical Lutheran Synod of Virginia (p. 7).

Olive Branch Synod, Forty-fifth Annual Convention Minutes (1893)

Treasurer's Report (p. 32): Richwoods, New Castle Charge, Pastor

Parochial Report (p. 36): Crossroads Richwoods Pastor

Synod of Kansas 35th Annual Convention Minutes (1893)

President's Report (p. 7): Rev. M. F. Rinker's letter of dismissal to the Synod of Virginia was returned to me, and one requested and returned to the Olive Branch, within whose bounds he had located.

East Ohio Synod, Fifty-ninth Annual Convention Minutes (1894)

Synodical Roll (p. 6): M. F. Rinker, Minister at Beach City, Ohio

Apportionment Report (p. 32): Beach City, M. F. Rinker with Navarre, Sherman's, St. James, and Beach City listed as his charge.

Parochial Report (p. 34): M. F. Rinker living at Beach City serving the following churches: Navarre (35 members, $1,000 church property value, $26 local expenses for all objects); Sherman (38,$500,$75.33); St. James (38, $1,300, $191.31); Beach City (39, $4,500, $225).

East Ohio Synod, Sixtieth Annual Convention Minutes (1895)
Parochial/Apportionment Report (p. 42): M. F. Rinker serving Navarre, Sherman, St. James, Beach City and supplying N. Industry.

Wittenberg Synod, Fiftieth Annual Convention Minutes (1896)
President's Report, New Members (p. 10): Rev. M. F. Rinker, from East Ohio Synod, Jan. 16, 1896

President's Report, Installations (p. 10): Rev. M. F. Rinker at Macomb, April 12, 1896.

President's Report, Dedications (p. 10): the corner-stone of the First English Lutheran Church at Macomb was laid with appropriate services August 30, 1896, conducted by the pastor, Rev. M. F. Rinker. The church is to be completed before winter.

Parochial Report (p. 48): M. F. Rinker, Macomb, serving Malinta and First English Lutheran at Macomb. (52/34, $3,000/$1,000, $310.50/$117).

Olive Branch Synod, Fiftieth Annual Convention Minutes (1897)
Roll of Synod (p. 6): M. F. Rinker, Ripple, Indiana

President's Report, Admissions (p. 8): Rev. M. F. Rinker was received from the Wittenberg Synod, September 7, 1897. He has been serving, as a supply, the Ebenezer charge for about three months.

President's Report, Miscellaneous (p. 9): On the 7th of October, 1897, the President visited the Highland Church, of the Ebenezer charge. A meeting was held, duly called, with this congregation, the councils of the other two churches belonging to this charge, and Rev. D. M. Horner, their former pastor. Some difficulties have existed of such a nature that do not really belong to the work of the Church, and should not affect it. One difficulty in the way to locate a pastor in the field, viz.: some salary due to their former pastor, was removed, and the way is open to locate a man in the field permanently. Rev. Rinker has been supplying East Salem and Pleasant View congregations of this same charge by special permission. It is hoped that the field may be occupied very soon.

President's Report, Vacancies (p. 10): The Ebenezer Charge has been supplied in part by Rev. M. F. Rinker. The time agreed upon as supplying has about expired.

Committee on Vacancies Report (p. 20): The Ebenezer Charge is composed of Peasant View, Highland, and East Salem. With the consent of the President of Synod, a part of this charge, namely, Pleasant View and East Salem, has been served by Rev. M. F. Rinker for almost three months past. The period during which the arrangement between Bro. Rinker and these two churches holds will expire within a few weeks. So far as we are informed, no effort is being made to settle a pastor, but all the congregations of the charge we are told are now ready to cooperate in such an enterprise.

Parochial Report (p. 31): M. F. Rinker, Broad Ripple, Indiana - serving Pleasant View, Highland, East Salem (30/41/32, $3,000/ $3,000/ $1,200, $87.18/$363.65/$37.35).

Olive Branch Synod, Fifty-first Annual Convention Minutes (1898)
Roll of Synod (p. 6): M. F. Rinker, Cross Roads, Indiana

President's Report, Miscellaneous (p. 9): 1. Rev. M. F. Rinker, who had been supplying the Ebenezer Charge, closed his labors in the field November 4, 1898. By special arrangement with

Rev. C. L. Kuhlman and the Grand View congregation, Rev. Rinker supplied the Grand View congregation from January 6, 1898, to July 17, 1898.

3. At the urgent request of Rev. C. L. Kuhlman, a visit was made to Rockport and Grandview, January 20, 1898. We held meetings with the councils of both congregations, the object being to come to a better understanding as to division of services between Rockport and Grandview, and also as to the support of the pastor. On account of bad roads and high waters at this time, not as much could be accomplished as I had desired. The arrangement between Rev. Kuhlman and Rev. Rinker was sanctioned. The congregations are now, as far as I know, harmoniously co-operating with each other.

Olive Branch Synod, Fifty-second Annual Convention Minutes (1899)

Vacancies (p. 9): Cedar Grove Church, Shepherdsville, Kentucky, has been without a pastor the entire year, but Rev. M. F. Rinker has been supplying them with the means of grace since November 1st.

Roll of Synod (p. 6) M. F. Rinker, Shepherdsville, Kentucky; absent and excused.

Committee on Vacancies Report (p. 24): The Cedar Grove Church has been supplied by Rev. M. F. Rinker since November 1st. We learn that this congregation is unable to support a pastor by itself, and it asks the Synod for aid in case they succeed in getting a pastor.

Parochial Report (p. 36): M. F. Rinker (supply) Cedar Grove, Shepherdsville, Ky (24, $1,000, $188.75).

Olive Branch Synod, Fifty-third Annual Convention Minutes (1900)

Roll of Synod (p. 6): Shepherdsville, Kentucky pastor

Report of Committee on Home Missions (p. 17): Cedar Grove Mission, Shepherdsville, Ky. Rev. M. F. Rinker, pastor. At the last meeting of Synod a special fund was raised by private subscriptions to aid this congregation to the amount of ten dollars a month in support of a pastor, in case they should secure one. The congregation secured the services of Rev. Rinker as regular pastor, and complied with the conditions of Synod. Your committee has secured thus far sufficient money to authorize the Treasurer to make the payments that were due. The pastor reports the work of the year very satisfactory; increased interest manifested in the services of God's house; and also in the improvement of the church property. Some of the young people seem to manifest quite an interest. Whilst there have been no accessions made during the past year, yet the young people that are growing up are reported to make accessible material for the near future. Rev. Rinker feels himself compelled to lay down the work in this field at the close of the year on account of the much travel on horseback, which he cannot endure, but thinks that the field should not be left without as pastor.

Treasurer's Report (p. 34)

Parochial Report (p. 38): 24 communicant members, $1,000 church property value, $291.81 local expenses for all objects.

Account of Synod Expenditures (p. 46): $100.00 to Pastor Rinker.

Olive Branch Synod, Fifty-fourth Annual Convention Minutes (1901)

President's Report, Dismissions (p. 7): Rev. M. F. Rinker, having accepted a call to Yutan, Nebraska. was dismissed July 5, 1901, to the Nebraska Synod.

President's Report, Vacancies (p. 7): The Cedar Grove Church, made vacant January 1, 1901, by the resignation of Rev. M. F. Rinker, succeeded in securing the services of Bro. C. E. Buschman as a supply, who began his services there May 26, 1901, and will continue to serve that church through the coming synodical year.

Nebraska Synod, Twenty-ninth Annual Convention Minutes (1902)

Parochial Report (p. 40): M. F. Rinker, Pastor, Yutan, Nebraska - Zion Evangelical English Lutheran Church at Yutan, and Zion Evangelical Lutheran Church at Roca, 19 and 20 communicant members respectively, $2,500 and $2,000 church property value respectively, $82.70 and $208 local expenses for all objects respectively.

Nebraska Synod, Thirty-first Annual Convention Minutes (1903)

Synodical Roll (p. 4): M. F. Rinker, (excused absence) Yutan, NE

Parochial Report (p. 44): M. F. Rinker, Yutan, NE , 18 members, $2,500 property value, $386.90 local expenses.

Nebraska Synod, Thirty-second Annual Convention Minutes (1904)

President's Report (p. 5): March 6, 1904, Rev. M. F. Rinker wrote he had resigned at Yutan, the same to take effect July 1. July 5th, 1904, Rev. M. F. Rinker was dismissed to the Rocky Mountain Synod, where he is engaged in mission work. Under Vacancies (p. 7): Yutan – we have a noble people, though the congregation is small. The contest for the possession of the parsonage had been decided in favor of the German congregation. This is a serious blow for our people.

Synod of Kansas, Thirty-eighth Annual Convention Minutes (1905)

President's Report, Accessions (p. 8): Rev. M. F. Rinker, from the Rocky Mountain Synod, February 9, 1905.

President's Report, Calls Accepted (p. 8): Rev. M. F. Rinker, Norcatur, Kansas, Feb. 1, 1905.

Parochial Report (p. 44): M. F. Rinker, Norcatur Charge – St. Mark's and St. Paul's Long Island (43/38, $2,500/$1,200/$202/$72.50).

Synod of Kansas, Thirty-ninth Annual Convention Minutes (1906)

Roll of Synod (p. 6): M. F. Rinker (excused absence) no notations

President's Report, Resignation (p. 7): Rev. M. F. Rinker, Norcatur, April 1, 1906

Synod of California, Seventeenth Annual Convention Minutes (1907)

No mention.

Synod of Kansas, Fortieth Annual Convention Minutes (1907)

Roll of Synod (p. 8): M. F. Rinker (excused absence) Los Angeles, California – no church given

Synod of Kansas, Forty-first Annual Convention Minutes (1908)

President's Report, Dismissals (p. 9): Rev. M. F. Rinker, California Synod, April 18, 1908

Synod of California, Eighteenth Annual Convention Minutes (1908)

Roll of Synod (p. 6): Michael F. Rinker, General Delivery

President's Report, Admissions (p. 7): Rev. Michael F. Rinker from Kansas Synod.

Home Missions Committee Report (p. 14): In February 1908, Rev. M. F. Rinker was authorized to supply the pulpit at Long Beach (Trinity?) until the pastor elect should arrive, his remuneration to be $5.00 a Sunday, one half of which is to be borne by Synod. He supplied them for seven Sundays.

Third Session Prayer (p. 17) Rev. M. F. Rinker offered prayer.

Synod of California, Nineteenth Annual Convention Minutes (1909)

Absences & Excuses Report (p. 14): M. F. Rinker sent a satisfactory excuse for not attending Convention.

Roll of Synod (p. 6): Michael F. Rinker, General Delivery (no church listed)

Synod of California, Twentieth Annual Convention Minutes (1910)

Synod Roll (p. 6): Michael F. Rinker at La Crescenta; entered Synod in 1906.

New Mission fields (p. 35): La Crescenta—Rev. M. F. Rinker is on mission duty at this place of 53 families (250 population), located about 12 miles northeast of Los Angeles. The town has a concrete church building, well adapted to religious needs, and owned by a man in Los Angeles. No other denomination is using it. There is no preaching point nearer than three miles. The chances for growth seem good.

Adjournment: Synod adjourned with prayer by Rev. M. F. Rinker (p. 36).

Synod of California, Twenty-first Annual Convention Minutes (1911)

Roll of Synod (p. 6): Michael F. Rinker (excused absence), Los Angeles, r258 West Temple St.

Home Missions Board Report (p. 22): La Crescenta-Rev. M. F. Rinker conducted services here from January 16 to August 7, 1910, covering a territory of nearly 20 square miles, with very little remuneration. Owing to the impossibility of securing a church property, Bro. Rinker retired from the field and the work was closed. For the same reason he declined to accept the aid voted by the Synod last year, and returned to the Treasurer of the Synod a check for $25.00, to which he was justly entitled. Your committee are of the opinion that this money should be repaid to Bro. Rinker.

Synod of California, Twenty-second Annual Convention Minutes (1912)

Synodical Roll (p. 6): Michael F. Rinker, Los Angeles, Glendale First

President's Report, Calls Accepted (p 10): Rev. M/ F. Rinker accepted the call to become pastor of the First E. L. Church of Glendale, which he had organized, and entered upon his pastorate September 1, 1912.

President's Report, Cong. Applications for Admission (p. 11): The First E. L. Church of Glendale, California, was organized by the adoption of a constitution recommended by our Board of Home Missions and the election of officers on Sunday, July 7, 1912. Twenty-six charter members were enrolled. The outlook is encouraging. The Rev. M. F. Rinker is the faithful, hard-working pastor. This congregation applies for admission into the Synod.

Home Missions Committee Report (p. 23): Your committee were also charged with having a canvass made of Glendale and vicinity and "a congregation organized if conditions warrant." The Rev. M. F. Rinker was engaged to make this canvass, with the result that on October 16, 1911, a Sunday School was organized and a week or two later a regular preaching service provided for. The Rev. M. F. Rinker has done faithful work for these people. On Sunday, July 7, they were organized into the First Evangelical Lutheran Church of Glendale. The congregation began with 26 charter members and an encouraging outlook. Rev. Rinker was elected pastor.

Parochial Report (p. 50): M. F. Rinker, Glendale First (27 members).

Synod of California, Twenty-third Annual Convention Minutes, (1913)

Synodical Roll (p. 6): Michael F. Rinker (excused absence) Glendale, 403 Brand Blvd., Glendale First

President's Report, Ministers Resigned (p. 8): On August 31, 1913, the mission at Glendale became vacant by the retirement of Rev. M. F. Rinker.

Home Mission Committee Report (p. 26): Glendale – This congregation was organized July 7, 1912, with 26 charter members, and has continued under the pastoral care of Rev. M. F. Rinker. The Sunday services have had an average attendance of 14 in the morning an 8 in the evening. The Sunday school attendance has averaged 21 and the prayer meeting 9. On account of a nervous breakdown, Brother Rinker requested to be relieved of the increasing demands of the congregation, and upon the expiration of his commission, August 31, he retired from the work. During the year a church lot was purchased for $1,150. Pledges amounting to $500 have been made, and $300 has been paid on the lot.

Parochial Report Summary

Greenleaf, Kansas	Trinity	1887	50	KS
Barnes, Kansas	Messiah	1887	19	KS
Washington, Kansas	St. Paul's	1888	42	KS
Washington, Kansas	St. Paul's	1889	46	KS
Minneapolis, Kansas	St. Paul's	1890	24	KS
Crossroads, Indiana	First	1892-93	66	ALM
Beach City, Ohio		1894	39	EO
Navarre	(Bethlehem)	1894	35	EO
St. James		1894	38	EO
Sherman		1894	38	EO
North Industry, Ohio		1895	—	EO
McComb, Ohio	First English	1896	52	WIT
Malinta, Ohio	Trinity	1896	34	WIT
Pleasant View, Indiana	English	1897	30	OB
Highland, Indiana	(Ebenezer)	1897	41	OB
East Salem, Indiana		1897	32	OB
Grand View, Indiana	St. Mark's	1898	44	OB
Rockport, Indiana	Trinity	1898	46	OB
Shepherdsville, Kentucky	Cedar Grove	1899-00	24	OB
Yutan, Nebraska	Zion	1901-03	19	OB
Roca, Nebraska	Zion	1902	20	OB
Cañon City, Colorado	Trinity English	1904	56	ALM
Norcatur, Kansas	St. Mark's	1905	38	KS
Long Island, Kansas	St. Paul's	1905	16	KS
Los Angeles, California	St. Mark's	1907/08	34	KS
Glendale, California	First	1912	17	CA

Membership represents "confirmand membership" in Parochial Reports.
Figures are taken from the Report available nearest to the time MFR served.

LUTHERAN ALMANAC AND YEARBOOK REFERENCES
(Lutheran Publication Society, Philadelphia, Pennsylvania)

YEAR	CHURCH TOWN	COUNTY	STATE	SYNOD
1886	Emporia	Lyons	Kansas	Kansas
1887	Greenleaf	Washington	Kansas	Kansas
1888	Greenleaf	Washington	Kansas	Kansas
1889	Washington	Washington	Kansas	Kansas
1890	Washington	Washington	Kansas	Kansas
1891	Minneapolis	Ottawa	Kansas	Kansas
1892	Orkney Springs	Shenandoah	Virginia	Kansas
1893	Crossroads	Delaware	Indiana	N. Ind.
1894	Beach City	Stark	Ohio	E. Ohio
1895	New Castle/Beach City	Stark	Ohio	E. Ohio
1896	Beach City	Stark	Ohio	E. Ohio
1897	McComb	Hancock	Ohio	E. Ohio
1898	McComb	Hancock	Ohio	E. Ohio
1899	Grandview	Spencer	Indiana	Olive Branch
1900	Shepherdsville	Bullitt	Kentucky	Olive Branch
1901	Shepherdsville	Bullitt	Kentucky	Olive Branch
1902	Yutan	Saunders	Nebraska	Nebraska
1903	Yutan	Saunders	Nebraska	Nebraska
1904	Yutan	Saunders	Nebraska	Nebraska
1905	Denver	Denver	Colorado	Rocky Mt.
1906	Norcatur	Decatur	Kansas	Kansas
1907	Santa Clara	Santa Clara	California	Kansas
1908	Los Angeles	Los Angeles	California	Kansas
1909	Los Angeles	Los Angeles	California	California
1910	Los Angeles	Los Angeles	California	California
1911	La Crescenta	Los Angeles	California	California
1912	Los Angeles	Los Angeles	California	California
1913	Glendale	Los Angeles	California	California
1914	Glendale	Los Angeles	California	California
1915	Glendale	Los Angeles	California	California
1916	Glendale	Los Angeles	California	California
1917	Glendale	Los Angeles	California	California
1918	Glendale	Los Angeles	California	California
1919	Glendale	Los Angeles	California	California
1920-1930	Los Angeles	Los Angeles	California	California

Index

Albright, Percy J. 89
Alexandria, Virginia 21
Allegheny Mountains 22
Altman, Frank D. .... 48f (pic), 51, 54, 57f, 76ff, 83
Altman, Josephine (Smith) 48f
American Danish Lutheran Church 64
Amsterdam 14
Appomattox, Virginia 7, 31, 40
Army of Northern Virginia 35, 40
Ashby District, Virginia .... 16 (pic), 17, 40f, 56
Ashby, Turner 30
Association of Evangelical Lutheran Churches 64
Augsburg Confession 64
Augustana Synod in North America 65

Baker, William 32
Barnes, Kansas 70, 82
Bassersdorf, CH 12f
Beach City Charge 70, 90f
Beach City, Ohio 17, 88ff
Beefsteak Raid 31
Belmont County, Ohio 42
Bering Land Bridge 19
Bethany Lutheran Church 94f
Blackwell, Oklahoma 71, 97
Bloody Angle Battle 9
Blue Ridge Mountains 21f
Book of Concord 64
Brandy Station Battle 31
Breckenridge, J. C. 8
Breite Chapel .... 13 (pic)
Broad Ripple, Indiana 91
Brown, John 10
Brownsburg, Virginia 34

Brownsville, Indiana 41
Bullitt County, Kentucky 95
Burruss, Warrick 21, 30

California 11, 71, 105
California Lutheran Hospital 115
California Synod 61, 66, 81, 106ff
Cannan, John 38
Canon City, Colorado 71, 97, 101f
Cedar Creek Battle 31, 34
Cedar Grove Mission 71, 94f
Champaign County, Ohio 40, 46
Children's Memorial Church (Kansas) 84
Christian Endeavor Society 91
Clark County, Ohio 41ff, 46f
Clarke County, Virginia ... 17, 25, 41ff, 46f
Colorado 101
Columbus, Ohio 43
Cowes (Isle of Wight) 14
Cumberland County, Maryland 45f

Dayton, Ohio 43
Deacons' responsibilities 76
Decatur, Indiana 70, 92
Delaware County, Indiana 70
Delia (slave) 25f
Depression Era 104
Diseases, shipboard 14
Dunkers and slavery 25

Early, Jubal 19, 31, 33
Earthquake (California) 106
East Ohio Synod 61, 90
East Salem Lutheran Church 91f
Ebenezer (Highlands) Lutheran Church 70, 91f
Emporia, Kansas 48, 54, 76ff, 83

Index | 147

Evangelical Lutheran Church
 in America 64f, 72
Evangelical Synod of Virginia 84
Fall Creek Township, Indiana 88
Finnish Evangelical Lutheran Church
 .... in America 65
First English Lutheran Church 70, 90
First Evangelical Lutheran Church ....
 (California)...................... 109, 113, 118
Fisher's Hill Battle 31
Florence, Colorado............................. 102
Flotz, Cordilla 114
Foltz. Elinor (Mrs. Joseph) 113
Foltz, John H. 113
Foltz, Mary (Mrs. John) 114
Foltz, Thomas....................................... 114
Forest Lawn Cemetery.......................... 116
Fraternal Lodges.................................... 64
Fredericksburg, Virginia 7, 34f
Fremont County, Colorado 101

Galloway, George N. 36
General Council............................... 65, 71
General Synod.................................... 65f
German language 12, 23, 61f, 99f
German Conference
 Nebraska Synod......................... 63, 65
German Evangelical Lutheran
 Synod 63f, 100

German Township, Ohio........................ 42
Germany 23, 26, 57, 61
Gezner, Hans Ulrich.............................. 13
Glendale, California.....59, 71, 108ff, 116, 118
Gold Rush in Colorado 102
Grace Reformed Church (Rinkerton).....56
Grandview, Indiana 71, 93f
Grant, U.S. 32, 35, 37
Graveltown Road 15
Great Warrior Path 19
Greenleaf, Kansas .... 70, 81f (pic)

Hamburg, Virginia................................. 56
Hamman, Alice..................................... 17
Hamman, Fannie.................................. 17
Hamman, Isaac 88
Hamman, Jacob 17
Hamman, Louisa................................... 88
Hamman, Rebecca 16f, 88
Hampshire/Hardy Counties,
 West Virginia.................................... 26

Hanover (Europe) 42
Hanover Junction, Virginia 8
Harper's Ferry, West Virginia................ 10
Harrisonburg, Virginia 22f
Heidelberg Catechism 23
Henkle, Socrates................. 34, 38, 50, 53f
Hesse-Darmstadt (Europe) 42
Holland (Europe)................................... 14
Holy Cross Lutheran Church 94
Home Mission Board 66, 81, 85, 99,
 107,117
Home Missions Commission 109f
Horner, D. M... 92
Howard's Lick Turnpike 21
Huber, D. B. 116

Indiana... 87
Indianapolis, Indiana...................... 62, 70
Indiana-Kentucky Synod....................... 61

Jackson, T. J. (Stonewall)................. 19, 29
Jefferson County, West Virginia............. 25
Jeffersontown Charge 95
Johnston, Virginia 26
Joint Synod of Ohio 70, 89
Jordan, Fannie 90
Jordan, J. W... 90

Kansas 43,104
Kansas Synod 61, 63, 66, 72, 97,
 101, 103, 106f
Kentucky-Tennessee Synod 95
Kremer, W. W. 76
Kuhlman, C. L. 93f

La Crescenta, California.............. 71, 108f
Lanham, Nebraska 64
Laurel Brigade 30
Lee, Robert E. 8, 24, 35, 37
Letter to editor .... 97f (pic)
Letter to Henkle................. 34, 38, 50, 53f
Letter from/to nephew 113f
Letter to parents 7ff
Letter to periodical............................ 103f
Lexington, Virginia 35, 40
Licensure for pastors........................... 79f
Licking County, Ohio 42
Little Church of the Flowers................ 116
Long Beach, California...................71, 108
Long Island, Kansas......................71, 103
Longstreet, James 8

148 | Michael F. Rinker: Pioneer Pastor

Los Angeles, California..59, 105f, 108, 111
Loudoun County, Virginia 26, 56
Lovettsville, Virginia 26, 54, 56
Lower Ebenezer Lutheran Church 92
Ludden, Luther P. 100, 102, 107f
Luray Valley, Virginia 22
Lutes, George W 95
Lutheran influences 51, 56
Lutheran Book of Worship 58
Lutheran Church in America 64f
Lutheran liturgy 58, 64
Lutheran Church–Missouri Synod 65
Lutheran/Reformed 52, 56f
Lutheran requirements 60, 62f
Lutherans and slavery 25

Madison, Township, Virginia 41
Mad River, Ohio 17, 43
Malinta, Ohio 70, 90f
Maryland 19, 21, 23, 42
Manasass Gap Railroad 21, 23
Massanutten Mountain 22
Mason County, Kentucky 26
Maphis, Indiana 33
McComb, Ohio 73, 91
McNulty, James 81
McPherson, Amy Semple 110, 116
Messiah Evangelical Lutheran Church 70, 82
Mill Creek 21f, 24
Middletown, Indiana 89
Minneapolis (Long Island), Kansas ...83f (pic)
Mittelberger, Gottlieb 13
Morning Star Lutheran Church 84
Mt Clifton, Virginia ... 7, 14f, 20ff, 32f, 35, 43, 47, 53, 57
Mt. Jackson, Virginia .. 8, 14f, 20ff, 30, 33f, 40, 54, 56

National Road (Cumberland Road) 42, 44, 47
Native Americans 18ff, 99
Navarre Lutheran Church 70, 89f
Nebraska population shift 99, 104
Nebraska Synod 61, 63, 66, 98
New Castle, Indiana 88
New Market, Virginia 8, 30, 53
Norcatur, Kansas .... 71, 97, 103 (pic)
North Industry, Ohio 70, 89
Northwestern Territory 47
Nuerensdorf, Switzerland 12

Ober, Henry 82
Ohio 16f, 87, 91
Oil discoveries 102, 109
Olive Branch Synod 61f, 66, 87, 91f, 94, 100
Ordination 80f
Orkney Grade 24
Orkney Springs, Virginia 15, 21, 70, 84

Painter Cemetery (Indiana) 17, 88f
Pastoral titles 49
Pastor's call 69
Pennsylvania 13f, 20, 23, 25, 42
Pennsylvania Volunteer Infantry (95th) ..36
Perry County, Ohio 42
Pike County, Ohio 42
Pine Church (Rinkerton) 56
Pittman, Levi 32, 36
Pleasant View Lutheran Church 70, 91f
Potomac River 18, 22
Powder Springs Lutheran Church 84
Preble County, Ohio 41

Quakers and slavery 25

Railroads 21, 23, 85, 95, 103
Ray, Nathaniel 13
Reck, Abraham 92
Reformed and Slavery 25
Rhine River 12f
Richmond, Virginia 7, 24, 35 37
Richwood (Crossroads) Church .... 17, 62, 70, 87ff (pic)
Ringger, Anna 14
Ringger, Barbara (Morff) 12
Ringger, Caspar 12
Ringger, Hans Jakob 12, 14, 41, 56
Ringger, Heinrich 12
Ringger, Jakob (father) 12
Ringger, Jakob (son) 12, 14
Ringger, Susannah 12, 14
Ringger, Ur 12
Rinker, Absalom 24, 25, 30
Rinker, Absalom (father) 10, 15f, 23f, 30, 35, 40, 42f, 46, 56, 61
Rinker, Albert M. 42
Rinker, Ann E. 41
Rinker, Anna 42
Rinker, Benjamin E. 31, 41f, 46
Rinker, Caroline 42
Rinker, Caspar 26

Index | 149

Rinker, Catharine (Weaver) 41
Rinker, Catharine 42
Rinker, Charles W 41
Rinker, Cloah 26
Rinker, Cora E 41
Rinker, Cynthia (Paddock) 41
Rinker, Elijah 26
Rinker, Elizabeth (Franz) 41
Rinker, Elizabeth (Snyder) 30
Rinker, Elnora 35, 116
Rinker, Emma E 41
Rinker, Ephraim 30
Rinker, Erasmus F 30
Rinker, Fenton T. 30
Rinker, George 26, 31, 41f
Rinker, Hannah 10, 31, 61
Rinker, Harry 41
Rinker, Henry St. John 21, 26, 30f,
54(pic), 56
Rinker, Henry 41
Rinker, Israel Putnam 30f, 56
Rinker, Jacob 41
Rinker, Jacob G 31
Rinker, Jacob Zwinglius 26
Rinker, Jefferson 41
Rinker, John 42
Rinker, John B. 41f
Rinker, John E. 41
Rinker, John H 88
Rinker, Jonathan 26, 30
Rinker, Joseph 41, 47
Rinker, Kora 40
Rinker, Levi 21, 24, 26
Rinker, Lydia 26
Rinker, Martha Jane (Burruss) 21
Rinker, Mary Ann 30
Rinker, Melinda 42
Rinker, Michael F.
  Church types 121f
  Grave marker .... 115 (pic)
  Housing 59, 123
  Obituary 60, 116ff
  Reimbursement 91, 101, 124
  Retirement 110, 113ff
  Travel 73, 95, 103, 124
Rinker, Minerva (Hamman) 10, 16, 21,
40ff, 46f, 51f, 56ff, 59, 85, 87f, 91, 116
Rinker, Minerva (death) .... 87, 89f (pic)
Rinker, Moses 26
Rinker, Nathaniel 15f, 30, 40, 42f, 115
Rinker, Noah F. 8, 30f, 40ff, 115f

Rinker, Osker 40
Rinker, Peter 41
Rinker, Philip 80
Rinker, Rachel 10, 30, 35, 40, 61
Rinker, Samuel W. 31
Rinker, Sarah (Branner) 41f
Rinker, Sarah J. (Sell) 40, 46
Rinker, Susan (Zirkle) 42
Rinker, Thomas J. 31
Rinker, Victoria 40
Rinker, William B. 42
Rinker's Store 24
Rinkerton, Virginia .... 15, 21ff (pic), 56
Roca, Nebraska 71, 98
Rockport Charge (Indiana) 71, 93f
Rocky Mountain Synod 66, 71, 100, 102f
Rosenberger, J. 33
Rotterdam, Netherlands 14

Salem Lutheran Church 115
Salem Township, Indiana 88
San Francisco, California 71, 104f
Santa Clara, California 71, 105
Secession Ordinance 28
Sharpsburg Campaign (Antietam) 31
Shenandoah County, Virginia 14f, 23ff,
28f, 36, 40
Shenandoah River 18, 20, 22
Shenandoah Valley 10, 16ff, 22, 24ff,
27ff, 35, 38, 46, 70, 87, 98, 104
Shepherdsville, Kentucky ... 59, 62, 71, 94f
Sheridan, Philip 19, 32
Sherman Lutheran Church 70, 89f
Slavery 25, 77
Snyder, Daniel 108
Spotsylvania Courthouse, Virginia 7, 10,
34f, 38, 77
Springfield, Ohio 17, 41ff, 46f, 50, 54,
57, 77
Springfield, Ohio, churches 47f
St. Andrew's Lutheran Church 106
St. James Lutheran Church 89f
St. John's Evangelical Lutheran
  Church 94, 97, 100f
St. Mark's Lutheran Church
  (California) 71, 77, 103, 106
St. Mark's Lutheran Church
  (Grandview) 71, 76, 93
St. Matthew's Lutheran Church 106
St. Oswald's Chapel (Breite) 12f
St. Paul's Lutheran Church 83f, 103

Stark County, Ohio 70
Staunton Light Artillery 30
Staunton, Virginia 23, 34, 84, 70, 90
Stockton, California 71, 105
Stonewall, Virginia 26
Strasberg, Virginia 22
Stuart, J. E. B 8
Switzerland 12, 23, 42, 57, 61

Teamsters (regimental) 9, 31, 37
Tennessee Synod 84
Toms Brook Battle 31, 33
Trinity English Evangelical
  Lutheran Church (Colorado)............ 102
Trinity Evangelical Lutheran Church
  (California) 108
Trinity Evan. Lutheran Church
  (Kansas) 71, 81f
Trinity Lutheran Church (Malinta) 90f
Trinity Lutheran Church (Rockport).... 93f

United Evangelical Lutheran Church 64
United Lutheran Church in America 65
United Synod of the South 65, 89
Upper Ebenezer Lutheran Church 92

Valley of Virginia 23f
Valley Turnpike (Route 11) 18, 21, 23
Vandalia, Illinois 45, 47

Virginia Cavalry, 12th Regiment 30f, 53
Virginia Cavalry, 7th Regiment 29
Virginia Convention, 1861 28
Virginia Military Institute 7, 35
Virginia Militia 29f
Virginia Synod 84
Wahoo, Nebraska 101
Wannamaker, Ulrich 106
Washington County, Kansas ... 70, 82f (pic)
Washington, D.C. 7, 21
Washington Township, Indiana 92
Waterville Lutheran Church (Kansas).... 70, 80
West Virginia 10, 25, 56
Wheeling, West Virginia 45
Whiteley, Fassler, & Kelly 44
Wilderness Campaign 7, 31, 35
Winchester, Virginia.... 19, 23, 25, 30ff, 42
Winterthur, Switzerland 12,
Wittenberg Lutheran College .. 50ff, 57, 98
Wittenberg Synod 61, 70, 90f, 98
Woodstock, Virginia 22, 26, 32
Wurtemburg (Europe) 42

Yutan, Nebraska ...... 71, 97, 100 (pic), 117

Zane's Furnace, Virginia 30
Ziegler, John M. 108
Zion Lutheran Church ... 97, 99ff 100 (pic)
Zurich, Switzerland 12ff, 23, 61